ALSO BY DIANE E. LEVIN

Remote Control Childhood? Combating the Hazards of Media Culture

Teaching Young Children in Violent Times:
Building a Peaceable Classroom

The War Play Dilemma: What Every Parent and Teacher
Needs to Know (with Nancy Carlsson-Paige)

Who's Calling the Shots? How to Respond Effectively to
Children's Fascination with War Play and War Toys
(with Nancy Carlsson-Paige)

Before Push Comes to Shove: Building Conflict Resolution Skills
with Children (with Nancy Carlsson-Paige)

From Conflict to Peace Building: The Power of Early Childhood
Initiatives—Lessons from Around the World
(with Paul Connolly and Jacqueline Hayden)

ALSO BY JEAN KILBOURNE

Can't Buy My Love: How Advertising Changes
the Way We Think and Feel
(originally published as *Deadly Persuasion*)

So Sexy
So Soon

BALLANTINE BOOKS | NEW YORK

So Sexy
So Soon

The New Sexualized Childhood

and What Parents Can Do

to Protect Their Kids

DIANE E. LEVIN, Ph.D.,

AND JEAN KILBOURNE, Ed.D.

Copyright © 2008 by Diane E. Levin and Jean Kilbourne

All rights reserved.

Published in the United States by Ballantine Books, an imprint of The Random House Publishing Group, a division of Random House, Inc., New York.

BALLANTINE and colophon are registered trademarks of Random House, Inc.

Library of Congress Cataloging-in-Publication Data
Levin, Diane E.
So sexy so soon: the new sexualized childhood and what parents can do to protect their kids / Diane E. Levin and Jean Kilbourne.
p.   cm.
Includes bibliographical references and index.
ISBN 978-0-345-50506-4
1. Children—United States—Social conditions.   2. Sex—Social aspects—United States.   3. Mass media and children—United States.   4. Sex in mass media.   5. Sex in popular culture—United States.   6. Body image in children—United States.   7. Body image in adolescence—United States.   8. Parent and child—United States.   I. Kilbourne, Jean.   II. Title.
HQ792.U56L48 2008
649'.65—dc22   2008023599

Printed in the United States of America on acid-free paper

www.ballantinebooks.com

2 4 6 8 9 7 5 3 1

First Edition

Book design by Jo Anne Metsch

To our children,
Eli Levin-Goldstein and Claudia Kilbourne Lux,
who continue to inspire, teach, and delight us

Contents

Contents

So Sexy
So Soon

Introduction

Changing Times, Changing Needs, Changing Responses

A four-year-old girl, in the dramatic play area of her preschool, begins swaying her hips and singing, "Baby, I'm your slave. I'll let you whip me if I misbehave." When her teacher goes over to talk to her about it, she volunteers that she learned the song from her eight-year-old sister. After doing a bit of research, the teacher discovers that the words are from a highly popular Justin Timberlake song.

Halloween costumes for young girls are so suggestive and risqué these days that Newsweek *runs a story titled "Eye Candy: Little Girls' Halloween Costumes Are Looking More Like They Were Designed by Victoria's Secret Every Year. Are We Prudes or Is This Practically Kiddie Porn?"*

A six-year-old casually asks at dinner, "What's a blow job?" Before his parents can respond, his ten-year-old sister knowingly screeches, "Oh my God, I can't believe he asked that!"

An eight-year-old boy comes home and reports to his father that he didn't know what to do when his friend showed him pornography on the Internet during a playdate at the friend's house.

3

Five students are suspended from their elementary school for sexual harassment stemming from an incident on a school bus that involved lewd language and touching. Some of the students said they were playing "the rape game."

A furor erupts at a bar mitzvah when two girls are caught performing oral sex on the thirteen-year-old bar mitzvah boy in a ladies' room stall.

Children as young as four learning to gyrate to songs in ways that might have stunned grown-ups a few decades ago. Elementary school children looking at pornography on the Internet and using words such as "rape" and "blow job." Young teens engaging in oral sex. Parents, grandparents, and teachers around the country and beyond tell us stories like these all the time—about how issues related to sex and sexuality come up in unexpected and even shocking ways with children, often at very young ages.

What's going on? Where does such behavior come from? What does it mean to and for children—and for the adults who care for them? Is it different from children's sexual behavior in the past, and if so, how? What are the implications for children's short- and long-term sexual development and behavior? And how should parents respond? This book will help you answer these pressing and vital questions and more.

WHAT'S THE PROBLEM?

Children growing up today are bombarded from a very early age with graphic messages about sex and sexiness in the media and popular culture. For instance, younger children have Bratz dolls, which surpassed the sales of Barbie dolls in 2006, and *Star Wars* action figures, which experience an explosion of sales of highly realistic violent toys every time a movie is released. As children get a little older there is the *Man-hunt II* video game, an extremely violent game that created a firestorm of protest upon its release for not carrying an A (Adult) rating that would have kept it from the hands of children and youth, and Victoria's Secret thong panties for tweens (eight- to twelve-year-olds) and teens.

Many industries make an obscene amount of money using sex and violence to market their products to children. Whatever their race, ethnic group, economic status, or gender, and whether they can afford to buy a lot or very few of these products, children are deeply affected. We have heard scores of stories, such as the ones above, about children who are learning to look and act in ways that disturb and even shock many adults. But these children are acting in ways that make perfect sense given the sexualized environment that surrounds them.

We are deeply worried. Children are paying an enormous price for the sexualization of their childhood. Girls and boys constantly encounter sexual messages and images that they cannot understand and that can confuse and even frighten them. Gender roles modeled for children have become increasingly polarized and rigid. A narrow definition of femininity and sexuality encourages girls to focus heavily on appearance and sex appeal. They learn at a very young age that their value is determined by how beautiful, thin, "hot," and sexy they are. And boys, who get a very narrow definition of masculinity that promotes insensitivity and macho behavior, are taught to judge girls based on how close they come to an artificial, impossible, and shallow ideal.

Both boys and girls are routinely exposed to images of sexual behavior devoid of emotions, attachment, or consequences. They learn that sex is the defining activity in relationships, to the exclusion of love and friendship. They learn that sex is often linked to violence. And they learn to associate physical appearance and buying the right products not only with being sexy but also with being successful as a person. Such lessons will shape their gender identity, sexual attitudes, and values, and their capacity for relationships, for love and connection, that they take into adulthood. While they struggle to make sense of all this, children are robbed of valuable time for age-appropriate developmental tasks, and they may begin to engage in precocious sexual behavior.

Children encounter these issues at much younger ages than in the past, long before they have the ability to understand or deal with them. One particularly heart-wrenching story recounted by the mother of a fourth-grade boy illustrates the kind of pain and suffering such messages can cause children (and their parents):

> My son has gotten three love letters from one little girl. He showed them to me and I could cry for this girl. She says, "I know I am not the prettiest girl or the thinnest girl but I love you and I just want you to love me." The rest of this letter is very grown up, about things they could do if they were boyfriend and girlfriend—which I don't feel I can share. But suffice it to say that they're ideas a nine-year-old never would have come up with even a few years ago. I've been in touch with the girl's mother, who is having a really hard time. I thought this must be an isolated event, a problem with this particular girl, but my son tells me that there are "couples" in the fourth grade. What is going on!? These letters are very recent and I am just beginning to unravel the issue with the school and other parents and children, who are just children for goodness' sakes!

The fourth-grade girl who wrote this letter is struggling with her inability to meet the *standard*. She has learned to talk about herself as if she were an object, judged solely by her looks. She has learned to be grown up beyond her years and to yearn for a romantic relationship with a boy. He, as many boys his age do, has to figure out how to deal with the sexy and provocative behavior of many of the girls in his life. The boy in the story above was fortunate to have a trusting relationship with his mother, so he could talk with her about his confusion. But in such a sexualized environment, how can we expect boys to learn how to have affectionate and caring relationships? Both girls and boys, but especially girls, are pushed into precocious sexuality in appearance and behavior long before they understand the deeper meaning of relationships or of the sexual behavior they're imitating.

WHAT THE PROBLEM IS NOT

We are not alarmed that today's children are learning about sex and sexuality. We are all sexual beings from birth, and this is to be celebrated. Children have always been curious about sex and sexuality from an early age, and it is good for parents and schools to give them honest and age-appropriate information. But what children are learning today isn't normal or good for them. We are alarmed by the particular lessons that children are learning. The sexualization of childhood is having a profoundly disturbing impact on children's understanding of gender, sexuality, and relationships.

WHAT'S NORMAL?

We want to be clear that sexualization is not the same as sexuality or sex. According to the *Report of the APA Task Force on the Sexualization of Girls* published by the American Psychological Association in 2007, sexualization has to do with treating other people (and sometimes oneself) as "objects of sexual desire . . . as things rather than as people with legitimate sexual feelings of their own." When people are sexualized, their value comes primarily from their sex appeal, which is equated with physical attractiveness. This is especially damaging and "problematic to children and adolescents who are developing their sense of themselves as sexual beings."

It is totally normal for children to go through a gradual process of coming to understand sex and sexuality, caring relationships, and intimacy, a process we pay close attention to in Chapter 3. When children are young, long before they can fully understand the meaning of sex and sexual relationships, the foundation is being laid for the kind of sexual relationships they will have when they grow up. It is built from their experiences, of course, both positive and negative. It encompasses the full range of these experiences, not just those that are directly about sex and sexuality. In fact, the first experiences that lay the foundation for positive ideas and values and emotions about sex aren't related to sex at all.

Ideally, children have direct personal experience being in and witnessing caring and affectionate relationships with family and friends. Ideally, they are nurtured by supportive and trusted adults, who are able and willing to answer questions and clear up confusion about issues such as the physical differences between males and females and the basics of making babies. These days, children also need to be able to talk with trusted adults about the relationships and sexual images that they see in the media and in the popular culture. *So Sexy So Soon* will give you lots of help in understanding how children process what they see, and ideas about how to have these conversations.

When children have many such opportunities, they progress much more successfully than they otherwise would. They are better able to cope with the inevitable stresses and strains of life. Over time, all this early learning helps them eventually become ready and able to establish a meaningful and intimate emotional and sexual relationship with a partner.

WHAT ISN'T NORMAL?

Sadly, today, instead of having the positive experiences they need for healthy development, many children are having experiences that undermine it. Today's cultural environment bombards children with inappropriate and harmful messages. As children struggle to understand what they see and hear, they learn lessons that can frighten and confuse them.

These lessons can seriously harm their ability to grow up to have healthy attitudes about themselves and their bodies and to have caring relationships in which sex is an important part. In the most extreme cases, the media's incessant sexualization of childhood can contribute to pathological sexual behavior, including sexual abuse, pedophilia, and prostitution. A 2003 *Newsweek* story on the rapid rise in teen prostitution in the United States reported that girls as young as nine are becoming involved. The majority of these girls are runaways or "throwaways," exploited by men who take advantage of their vulnerability and desperation.

Child sexual abuse occurs at an alarming rate. According to the most reliable studies, as many as one in three girls and one in seven boys will be sexually abused at some point during their childhood. Almost 90 percent of the time, the abuser is someone known, and often loved and trusted, by the child. Many abusers convince themselves that the child is "asking for it" and enjoys it. The sexualization of childhood encourages these dangerous attitudes and makes it seem normal to look upon children as sex objects. While child sexual abuse is beyond the scope of this book, the sexualized climate we describe most likely contributes to it.

When sex in the media is talked about, it is often criticized from a puritanical perspective—there's too much of it, it's too blatant, it will encourage kids to be promiscuous. But sex in commercial culture has far more to do with trivializing and objectifying sex than with promoting it, more to do with consuming than with connecting. The problem is not that sex as portrayed in the media is sinful, but that it is synthetic and cynical. The exploitation of our children's sexuality is in many ways designed to promote consumerism, not just in childhood but throughout their lives.

Until recently, the sexualization of childhood and its impact on children has primarily been the focus of the Christian right. This group generally uses moralistic arguments to condemn the current social climate and to insist that abstinence-only sex education will solve the problem. The issue has been largely ignored by the wider society be-cause many adults have become desensitized or feel ill prepared to deal with it. Even the best-intentioned and best-prepared parents often feel helpless to protect their children from the onslaught.

In the past couple of years, this denial and avoidance have begun to change. For example, the *Report of the APA Task Force on the Sexual-ization of Girls* mentioned earlier led to significant attention to the issue by the media when it was released in February 2007. This is heartening, but we still have a very long way to go. The focus of public concern so far is primarily on adolescence, not on early childhood. But early childhood is when the foundation is laid, and that is where we need to start our efforts to understand and respond. Almost all of the attention that has been given to this issue focuses on girls. Girls suffer more overtly and perhaps more deeply, but boys suffer too. And boys raised in a sexualized culture often become men who are unsatisfying and sometimes even dangerous partners for women. No discussion of how to protect children from sexualized childhood would be complete without discussing how to meet the needs of boys. And finally, we want to acknowledge that while there is not necessarily a great disparity in rich and poor children's exposure to the sexualized environment, the huge economic disparities in today's society can have a profound im-pact on how they participate in it.

A SHARED JOURNEY

The seeds for writing this book began at the Feminist Expo 2000 in Baltimore, Maryland. That was the first time the two of us worked to-gether professionally. We gave a presentation on the challenges and dangers of raising children in today's gender-biased world. At our session, Diane mapped out the extreme gender divisions, stereotypes, and increasing violence and sexualization that saturate marketing and media directed at children. She argued that these stereotypes and media messages limit opportunities for children to develop as whole people and undermine the very foundation necessary for children to actualize their full potential and to value and respect themselves and others. Jean then illustrated how these images and marketing messages aimed at younger children gradually evolve into the images and messages prevalent in the tween and teen popular culture. She showed how the harmful lessons learned by the younger children often lead to serious problems in later years, such as increasing objectification of women (by both women and men), eating disorders and depression, and even sexual violence. By the time Jean was done, there was a lot of distress in the room.

When we spoke in Baltimore, we both had already spent decades studying, teaching, and speaking publicly to students, parents, and professionals in many fields about how media and commercial culture affect children's and adolescents' development. Diane's work had always focused on preschool and elementary children. In the mid-1970s she taught a course on sexism in education, which focused on how sexism in society limits the potential of both girls and boys and what schools can do about it. Jean began examining the image of women in advertising in the late 1960s. Around the same time that Diane taught her course, Jean made the first version of her highly acclaimed film *Killing Us Softly: Advertising's Image of Women* and launched her career as a lecturer on this and related topics.

We had worked for years to promote the optimal development of both girls and boys. But Jean had not known very much about the foundation being laid in childhood and the extreme measures used by marketers to exploit children. Diane had not focused on what happened to children as they entered adolescence and then adulthood. We were educated and fascinated by each other's work and saw the power that came from putting the pieces together.

A few years later, as our concern about what we saw happening to children and teenagers all around us deepened, we decided to do some work together. We began talking with parents (and teachers) about how the experiences they were having with children related to sexualized childhood. When word got out that we were collecting these stories, many parents with stories to share contacted us. These parents were struggling to raise their children in a toxic cultural environment. They were upset. They were outraged. They wanted reassurance, and above all they wanted help.

As our story collection grew and we met more and more parents desperate for information, we knew that we had to write this book. However, after talking to parents and working on the book together for over a year, we realized that the focus should be on early childhood. Increasingly, this is when the problems of the new sexualized childhood begin. And there are far fewer resources available to help the parents of younger children deal with this than there are for the parents of older children. At this point, Diane became the lead author, with primary responsibility for the material dealing with young children, and Jean took primary responsibility for the material dealing with tweens and adolescents.

HELP IS ON THE WAY!

We wrote *So Sexy So Soon* because children desperately need your help and we want to help you give it to them. Most parents know something is terribly wrong. But it isn't easy to connect all the dots between the experiences you are having with your children and what is going on in the culture, never mind figuring out what to do about it once you make the connections. This book will connect the dots. As you read, you will develop a lens that will help you see more clearly how the graphic sexual messages that permeate the lives of your children—both girls and boys—are harming them in ways that go far beyond what they're learning about sex. Once you have that lens, we'll show you how it can help you find ways to protect your children. You will also see that you are not alone! Parents and professionals everywhere are struggling to deal with this new sexualized environment and often feel confused about how best to respond.

The primary focus of *So Sexy So Soon* is on children, girls and boys, from preschool through the tween years. This is when the foundation is laid for later sexual behavior and relationships. This is when you can make the biggest difference in reducing the negative impact of the sexualization of childhood on your children. We also show you how what you do in the early years paves the way for staying connected with your children when the stakes get higher in adolescence.

It's important to acknowledge that there are variations in how children are affected by today's sexualized childhood—based on their gender and their racial, cultural, and socioeconomic group as well as their individual disposition. And children's marketers actually use sophisticated techniques to target different demographic groups. We wish we had enough space to go into all these variations in this book, but we don't. Nonetheless, *So Sexy So Soon* is relevant for all children, because the ways in which kids internalize the messages are very much the same, and no child growing up today can fully escape today's sexualized environment.

We want to make you a promise. It's not fair that your job is made so much harder than it needs to be by the sexualized media and commercial culture. Society should support you in your efforts rather than set up roadblocks at every turn. If society supported parents in their job, we wouldn't need to write this book. Too often you, the parents, are told that the problem of sexualized childhood is your fault: If you were doing your job right and could just learn to say no, then there wouldn't be a problem. Casting blame on parents is a smoke screen that diverts attention from where the blame rightfully belongs—squarely on the shoulders of the purveyors of these media and marketing messages, those who exploit our children's developmental vulnerabilities by using sex to make huge profits.

We promise to keep the blame squarely where it belongs. Without promising that *So Sexy So Soon* will help you solve all the problems you and your children face, we will help you find many ways you can make life a whole lot better for your children (and for you) than it otherwise might be. And while we will help you banish many of the evils that the sexualized childhood creates in your children's lives, we will not ask you to banish all of them. Rather, we will show you how to work with the evils that do get in and transform them into positive lessons for your children. We will show you how to help your children expand their horizons in ways that respect who they are as individuals.

Finally, we apologize in advance for how distressing you may find the first part of this book. Today's sexualized childhood *is* very distressing, there's no way around that. We believe that understanding and action are the best antidotes to the alarm this content will cause. Using the understanding you develop, you will learn what you can do to take action to make a difference in your children's lives, perhaps even in the lives of all children. We will show you in detail how to do this in the second part of the book. Protecting and building resilience in your children will not be easy. But it is our goal that by the time you have finished reading *So Sexy So Soon*, you will feel empowered by having the knowledge and skills you need to effectively and caringly help your children navigate the sexualized minefields of our culture. You will feel prepared to help your children grow up sexually healthy and whole— to survive and thrive, even in today's sexualized world.

Chapter 1

Never Too Young to Be Sexy

Living with Children in Today's Sexualized World

It has never been easy being a parent. But today, it has gotten even more difficult. A 2002 survey by an organization called Public Agenda found that 76 percent of parents felt it was a lot harder to raise children today than when they were growing up, and 47 percent reported that their biggest challenge was trying to protect their children from negative societal influences, including disturbing and confusing images, violence, and age-inappropriate messages appearing in the media.

How would you have answered this survey? Are you, too, having a hard time trying to protect your children from negative influences? Are you finding it difficult to set and enforce limits on the media that your children are exposed to—to determine how much, when, and what? As parents, you are often told that it's your job to "just say no" to all of the inappropriate content out there, and that this will solve the problem. But just saying no won't solve the problem, and anyway, you can't say no to everything!

Instead, we simply have to deal with the popular culture in our children's lives, often at the most unexpected times, in unforeseen ways, and whether we want to or not. This book is designed to help you do just that. And in order to be able to do so, the first order of business is to examine and recognize when and how the new sexualized childhood is influencing children from a young age.

Several recent books and news and research reports have expressed concern about today's sexual attitudes and behavior of many adolescents, and increasingly even tweens (eight- to twelve-year-olds). These accounts often make it seem as if the behavior in question suddenly appears out of a vacuum when children enter high school (or middle school). Rarely do we hear about what was happening in the early years that paved the way for what is happening with teens.

There is a lot going on in children's lives around issues of sexuality and sexiness that is important for the caring adults in their lives to recognize. The following stories from parents and teachers make it very clear that if we are to understand and deal with the sexualization of childhood, we must begin our efforts with very young children.

CRYING IN THE BATHTUB

Jennifer reported that one evening not long ago, her seven-year-old daughter Hannah began crying in the bathtub. Alarmed, Jennifer asked what was wrong. Hannah responded, "I'm fat! I'm fat! I want to be pretty like Isabelle—sexy like her! Then Judd would like me too!" Jennifer knew Isabelle, a very thin, very popular girl in Hannah's class who wore "stylish" clothes that Jennifer thought were inappropriate for a seven-year-old. Jennifer put her hand on Hannah's shoulder and said she liked Hannah's body—it was a wonderful body for a seven-year-old and she certainly didn't need to lose weight. But Hannah continued to cry and to say that she wanted to go on a diet. Jennifer felt uncertain about what to say or do next. In her view, Hannah had a normal body for a seven-year-old girl. Jennifer thought it must be abnormal for such a young child to be thinking about diets, let alone wanting boys to like her for being "pretty" and "sexy." But, normal or not, Jennifer saw that Hannah was truly concerned and distressed, and she wanted to do something to help.

As Jennifer strove to understand Hannah's outburst, she was tempted to put a lot of the blame on Hannah's friends, who were becoming increasingly influential and important to her. Recently, Hannah had come home from a playdate talking about having had a fashion show with her friend's Bratz dolls. Jennifer was concerned that when Hannah and her friends played together they often acted out going on "dates" and having weddings with their Barbie dolls, but she was truly horrified by the time they spent at other houses with Bratz dolls—by their name, their anorexic-looking bodies, their overt sexuality and hookerlike wardrobe, as well as by the focus on shopping and appearance as the point of the play. When she voiced her reservations about Hannah's having the dolls, Hannah said that everyone else had them and that she loved playing with them at other children's houses. She and her friends liked dressing them up and having them go shopping and out on dates. Although Jennifer didn't give in, she wasn't sure what she would do when Hannah's birthday arrived the following month. She was certain some other girls would give these dolls to Hannah as gifts. Even if Jennifer took them away, she knew Hannah would continue to play with them at her friends' homes. Recently, Hannah had begun to nag about joining the Bratz website, an online community where kids can play and buy things for their Bratz dolls in cyberspace, along with other children who are logged on.

Deep down, however, Jennifer realized that what worried her most was where this interest in appearance, popularity, and sexiness would lead. If Hannah was dissatisfied with her body at the age of seven, she wondered how she might feel at thirteen. Jennifer had seen news stories about an increase in precocious sexual behavior among children and teens, and she knew that eating disorders were on the rise, even among little girls. Were Hannah's tears about her body the first sign of such trouble for her? What was the relationship between concerns about body image and sexuality? And what did she mean by being "sexy" anyway? Knowing how high the stakes were, Jennifer felt almost desperate to find the right way to respond. But she was upset with herself for feeling unsure, even anxious, about knowing the right thing to say or do.

PROFESSIONAL WRESTLING GIRLS

Nora, a highly experienced kindergarten teacher, told us about an incident with a child that left her scrambling to figure out how to respond. In his daily school journal, five-year-old James had made a drawing of what looked to Nora like a woman, with long hair and bright red lips as well as big wavy circles on her chest that looked like breasts. Next to the drawing he had written the letter *W* over and over again. Nora asked him to tell her about his picture. She was caught off guard when James explained that his drawing was of "a professional wrestling girl with big boobies."

"At first I thought he was trying to be fresh, to be a wise guy, but I caught myself before I reacted too harshly," Nora reported. "I took a deep breath and tried to think through how to respond. I decided to start with a question." (This is almost always a good way to start when you're not quite sure what to say.) So Nora asked James what he knew about "wrestling girls." He matter-of-factly replied with his eyes open wide, "I saw her on TV last night with my [big] brother, Brett. He was babysitting! He let me stay up late and watch with him! It's a secret!" She was glad she had asked him the initial question about what he knew about wrestling girls, because his response helped her begin to get a handle on what was going on for James.

Nora recalled that it was the look on James's face when he answered her, of both bravado and worry at the same time, that left her confused and concerned. She knew that James's parents were quite clear about limiting the amount and kind of media in his life. She knew how much James looked up to fourteen-year-old Brett and admired everything he did. She was pretty sure that James's parents would be distressed if they knew about Brett and James's secret! She was also pretty sure that if James shared the secret with her, he was asking for something, but what exactly was it?

Rather than try to work it all out with James at that moment, Nora decided to buy some time to think about what to do. So she said to James, "It sounds like you saw things you hadn't seen before . . . things that were not really for kindergartners. I'm glad you told me about your secret." James smiled and put his journal away.

After the event was over, there was a lot for Nora to consider. Why did James decide to disclose the secret to her and do it through his daily journal? Why did he choose to focus on the breasts? Did he know that focusing on them could be seen as provocative to his teacher or have sexual connotations? After all, what signifies sex to an adult might mean something quite different to a five-year-old. Was James trying to use his drawing to brag and feel more grown up about his having seen this grown-up program? Or could he have made his drawing because he needed someone to talk to about it when he knew he couldn't reveal it to his parents because it was a secret? Was he testing Nora to see if she would get upset or angry, or looking to her to help him sort the experience out?

Nora began to think about the issue more broadly than just about James. If James drew his picture of the "professional wrestling girl" as a way of talking to an adult about something disturbing he saw on the screen, as Nora now thought he did, do other children also need such opportunities to process the graphic content they are seeing in media and popular culture? Well, then, whom are they talking to? How often do children end up seeing things their parents don't want them to see and then learn not to talk to adults about it? And when they do experience the forbidden fruit, what does it teach them about honesty and deceit and about the nature of their relationship with the important adults in their lives?

Finally, Nora started to feel better about how she had responded to James and realized she had learned an important lesson for her future teaching: Whether they're scared or want to feel grown-up and impress others with what they've seen, this is the kind of conversation with an adult that children often need in order to help them deal with the sex and violence they see. Furthermore, such conversations might also be used to teach children alternative lessons to what they're learning from the screen.

But Nora didn't leave it there. She began to think about what should happen beyond the classroom. What should the role of schools be in helping children (and their parents) deal with the sexualized media culture? How was this experience with James related to debates that were raging around the country about whether to teach sex education—and, if so, what kind and when? More particularly, did she have a responsibility to talk with James's parents about the professional wrestling girl episode? If she did talk to them, would this upset James and make him feel he couldn't trust teachers and other adults to help him deal with scary secrets next time? Or would speaking with the parents help them connect more positively with James so that it would be easier for him to use them next time, rather than his teacher, to talk about what he'd seen on TV?

Nora was aware of a 2006 Kaiser Family Foundation report that found that many children spend more time involved with media than on anything else but sleeping. So why wasn't media education part of the school curriculum? Why didn't schools see that they have a vital role to play in helping to influence the lessons that media are teaching children? Was the push to teach the "basics" for standardized tests that came from the federal government's "No Child Left Behind" mandate crowding out content that children urgently needed to work on? If children didn't have avenues to deal with their feelings about media content, what happened to these feelings? Did their involvement with the disturbing and confusing images and behaviors they saw distract them from giving their all to traditional schoolwork?

While there was not one right or easy answer to most of Nora's questions, she realized that the increasing exposure of the children in her classroom to confusing sexual content was creating new challenges for her that she needed to take seriously. We need more teachers like Nora in today's world!

"WHAT'S A BLOW JOB?"

Meghan recounted with obvious distress that her seven-year-old daughter, Eva, had come home from school the day before and asked, "Mom, what's a blow job?" Meghan's first impulse was to tell Eva that it wasn't something for children, it was for adults, and to terminate the conversation then and there. But something about the earnest expression on Eva's face made Meghan pause. "Stay calm, stay calm!" she told herself. Then she asked, "Where did you hear about blow jobs?" Eva replied that she heard about it at school. Meghan followed with, "What did you hear about it?" Eva responded, "It's sex." Meghan couldn't imagine where to go next with the conversation.

Meghan had always tried to protect Eva from exposure to violence and sex in the media. But ever since Eva had entered a large elementary school with many children who were not as protected as Eva, Meghan felt she was increasingly losing her ability to control this exposure. This new episode left Meghan feeling that things were really out of control. She had been aware, with some degree of ambivalence, that she might need to talk with Eva about issues such as oral sex during the adolescent or even the preadolescent years. She had heard news reports about incidents of oral sex in high schools. She had read that several boys at a private school near Boston were expelled because a girl had performed oral sex on all of them in the locker room. More recently, a friend had told her that two girls at a bar mitzvah had performed oral sex on the bar mitzvah boy in a bathroom. She certainly was disturbed by these incidents, but she was utterly appalled that the subject had come up with Eva at age seven!

Meghan and her husband had talked about how they wanted to be open and comfortable with Eva when talking about sex. But they had expected Eva's first questions to be about where babies come from, not this. This was simply not what they had had in mind! Should Meghan actually describe oral sex? What could this possibly mean to a seven-year-old? And how would her explanation affect Eva's understanding about sex and relationships between caring adults, both short and long term? Meghan also didn't know what to think about the children who had used the term "blow job" in Eva's presence. Where were they getting this language? What did they know?

You might think that Meghan's experience is an aberration. Initially we thought so too. It certainly isn't an everyday experience that parents have with their children. But when we shared this story with a group of parents at a workshop, a father excitedly (and seemingly with relief) raised his hand and said, "The same thing happened with my son. He's eight and last week he came home from school asking, 'What does it mean to "suck your dick"?' I figured we were the only family dealing with this. That's why we came to your talk tonight!"

SEXUAL HARASSMENT AT AGE FIVE?

Jason got into trouble one day when his kindergarten classmate Ashley came home from school and reported to her parents that Jason had told her that he wanted to "have sex" with her. Ashley's parents, very upset, told her she should never play with Jason again, that he was a bad boy. They then contacted the teacher and the principal and demanded a meeting with Jason's parents. All of the adults involved were concerned about what might be going on in Jason's home for him to come up with such a comment at the age of five. In some circumstances, such comments from young children can be an indication of sexual abuse. The principal, a firm believer in the school's Zero Tolerance policy that said any child who committed an act of aggression or violence was subject to suspension, was considering a brief suspension to teach Jason that he should never say such a thing.

Fortunately for little Jason, the school psychologist met with him before this could happen. She told him that some people were worried about what he said to Ashley. She asked him if he would tell her what he said and what he had wanted to do to Ashley. Jason instantly burst into tears. He sobbed, "I wanted to kiss her. I like her. I like her." This was the first time anyone had bothered to ask Jason what he meant by what he said, a potentially damaging error on the part of the adults. They were all using an adult lens for interpreting what he said about sex, not a child's lens. Often when adults think "sex," children have something very different on their minds.

An important question to ask in this situation is to what degree Jason's comment grew out of his efforts to make sense of the messages about affection, sex, and relationships that he might be getting every day from popular culture. While it is hard to answer this question in hindsight, in these times it's probably safe to assume that the popular culture could very well have played a significant role. Had it not been for the school psychologist, he might have been punished for doing something he'd learned and internalized from those messages. Jason, as much a victim of the sexualized popular culture as Ashley, was also victimized by the adults' fear and misunderstanding.

We can only be grateful that the psychologist found a way to connect with Jason, to hear his point of view. We can hope that Jason got the kind of support he needed to regain his self-confidence and to learn how to express affection for his peers in appropriate ways. We also hope that Ashley got help working through the misguided and disturbing response she got to Jason's words from the adults around her.

A highly publicized story about a first-grader in the Boston area did not have such a happy ending. A boy was suspended from school for a week when a girl in his class reported that he touched her skin inside the waistband of the back of her pants. The Zero Tolerance policy in his school left no room to take into account the understanding or possible needs of this seven-year-old child. Once again, here is a child paying a high price for the new sexualized childhood and adults' reaction to it. And both stories illustrate a very disturbing trend—as adults get more and more uptight about how the sexualized environment is affecting children, they end up ascribing adult intent to behaviors that would have been interpreted as "children just being children" in the past.

PREMATURE ADOLESCENT REBELLION

The big topic of conversation for Tessa's eighth birthday was the upcoming party—a sleepover with her three best friends and a magic show for entertainment. Tessa and her father had been learning magic tricks together and Tessa was excited about this new skill. Both parents were enthusiastic about the magic show too, since they had been afraid Tessa would want to show her birthday guests a DVD for entertainment. It was always a problem to choose an appropriate one. At the party, the magic show was a big hit, and Tessa taught her appreciative friends how to do the tricks. But later in the evening the bubble burst for the parents.

After ice cream and cake, the girls retired to Tessa's bedroom to get ready for bed. About a half hour later Tessa's mother, Kate, quietly went into the hallway to see how they were doing. Through the bedroom door, left slightly ajar, she overheard a conversation that took her breath away. The girls were talking about what Cassie, a girl in their class who was not at the party, had worn to school that day—a midriff shirt that exposed her belly button. Kendra said, "My mom says I can't have one. I keep telling her it's not fair." MacKenzie said without hesitation that her mom let her choose the clothes she wanted and Kendra's mom was really mean for not letting Kendra choose her clothes. Emily agreed. Tessa seemed not to be participating much. As Kate continued to eavesdrop, she learned that "the boys like Cassie." They chase her on the playground, and one of the boys actually ran up to her and kissed her! Kate also learned that the boy is Cassie's "boyfriend" now, and he likes her because she's "sexy."

The girls talked on and on—about how it wasn't fair that Cassie got to wear whatever she wanted. Even MacKenzie and Emily, who had shirts that showed off their belly buttons, complained that they couldn't wear them to school. Furthermore, the girls then discussed how they could get their parents to let them wear these shirts to school. MacKenzie and Emily gave Tessa and Kendra advice about how they could bypass their parents by getting their grandparents to buy them belly button shirts. All the girls agreed that grandparents often buy things that parents won't buy.

MacKenzie boasted that she had seen a copy of the magazine *CosmoGIRL!* at her teenage cousin's house. It showed really skinny models wearing really short belly button shirts that were "*sooooo* cool." There was even an article on dieting. This led Tessa to pipe up, proudly announcing that she was on a diet and that she was going to be really skinny. The other girls said they were going to go on diets too. Kate wondered how Kendra, who was in fact somewhat overweight and had fallen strangely silent, felt about this discussion.

Kate was stricken. She was appalled that eight-year-olds were thinking and talking about such things. She thought that such topics—worrying about being sexy, skinny, and popular with boys and trying to figure out how to trick parents—didn't emerge until early adolescence at twelve or thirteen. She wanted to barge into the bedroom and tell the girls that they were far too young to have such concerns. She wanted to tell them to go to sleep! But rationally Kate knew that even if she did march in to voice her concerns, the issues raised in the girls' conversation would not go away. Rather, they would just stay underground as the girls continued to try to understand these issues beneath the radar of critical adults.

Many questions were spinning around in Kate's head, none very comforting. First, she wondered about the girls' envy of Cassie and their desire to be "sexy" and popular with boys, like her. Weren't the girls a little young to be thinking about themselves and their peers in terms of sexiness bringing popularity? They were talking about one another and Cassie as if they were objects who would be judged entirely by their looks and whether or not their clothing was sexy. Second, Kate was concerned about the seemingly strong peer pressure in the group to look a certain way and to judge themselves and one another by their success in that narrow effort.

But Kate was most upset that the children were talking about adults, their parents, as if they were "the enemy," opponents who prevented them from buying and wearing what they needed to be happy and successful. This seemed like adolescent behavior to her. Of course, one of the developmental tasks of adolescents is to separate from their parents and become more independent as friends and peers play increasingly important roles. Kate understood this in theory. But weren't these children a bit young to be starting their adolescent rebellion? Was this a *premature adolescent rebellion*? Was this the *age compression* she had heard about, where issues that used to be of relevance to older children were moving down to younger and younger children?

LEARNING ABOUT SEX FROM THE INTERNET

Connie teaches health education to the fifth- and sixth-grade children in her school. By the time the children get to these grade levels, they are generally quite comfortable discussing personal topics with Connie and with one another. Still, she meets with the boys and girls separately a couple of times during the sex education course, because this helps them be more open to discussing uncomfortable issues related to sexuality. Several years ago, a comment from one of the boys in the boys-only session gave Connie reason to be concerned. She had been talking with the boys about the idea of sex occurring in a relationship as an expression of deep affection between the sexual partners, when a boy named Gabe jumped in and challenged her by saying, "Well, I think you *don't* need to like the person. I saw sex on the Internet. My cousin showed me. They just do it 'cause it's fun, they like it." A couple of boys seemed surprised, but a few others said that they had seen it too and that Gabe was "right."

On the one hand, Connie was upset that some of the boys had access to pornography on the Internet. On the other hand, she considered it a positive sign that Gabe had felt comfortable enough to raise the issue with her, and that other boys in the class seemed interested in the topic. Clearly it had been very much on their minds and they really wanted to talk about it. But how did this comment of Gabe's affect one of the most basic lessons she had always tried to teach the children—that sex is a special part of a relationship between caring adults? Even though she was a veteran teacher and expert in this area, Connie was stumped for the right response to comments like Gabe's.

In subsequent years, and because of the now ubiquitous access to the age-inappropriate content on the Internet that many kids are exposed to, Connie decided to change her approach to her first boys-only session. "Early on I ask them what they have seen about sex on TV, in movies, or on the Internet. Last week, every boy raised his hand when the issue of having seen 'sex' and pornography on the Internet came up. When I probed to find out more about what they saw, it was clear that two or three of them hadn't seen real pornography, but I think all the others had! The times have changed very rapidly since Gabe first raised the issue of pornography on the Internet in my class, and the issue certainly adds a whole new dimension of complexity to the work that I do." Connie's realization that she had to bring the media and popular culture into her discussions about sex was an important breakthrough. As she began doing this, what Connie learned about how to lead such discussions (described in Chapter 6) can help us all become better able to talk with children about the sex they are exposed to in media and popular culture.

MEETING THE CHALLENGE

Did any of these parents' and teachers' stories sound familiar? As you read, what kinds of reactions did you have? You might be asking, "What's happening to the world? This would never have occurred when I was their age." Do you wonder what might be going on with your own children that you don't even know about regarding sexual issues? Are you thinking, "How is all this going to affect my children's healthy sexual development as they are growing up? If children at five, six, and seven years old are doing things like this, what will be going on when they are tweens and adolescents?" Or perhaps you feel angry, not with the children who are struggling to understand sex and sexuality, but at the world that contributes so negatively to these struggles. Do you wonder how it got to be like this? Do you worry about what you can and should do?

Each of these stories has a lot to do with sex and sexuality. But they also have implications—that go far beyond sex—for children's overall development, attitudes, and behavior. For example, we see the beginning of a premature adolescent rebellion as young girls try to figure out how to trick their parents into buying them sexy clothes so they will be popular with the boys. We see a clash of cultures between parents and the media as ten-year-old boys learn lessons about sex from the Internet that undermine the lessons about sex in the context of loving relationships that caring adults are trying to teach. We also see examples of the objectification of oneself and others as both girls and boys learn that how you look rather than who you are determines the value others place on you. Unfortunately, it's not a very big leap from this kind of objectification to a range of unhealthy emotional consequences such as eating disorders and depression.

There have always been changes in society from one generation to the next. Parents have always noticed how their children's world differs from the world of their own childhood. But what is happening now regarding sex and sexuality in the media and popular culture goes far beyond the changes that have occurred between other generations in the past. A revolution is taking place that we need to take seriously. It is a revolution that is harming our children and harming the wider community. We must understand this new world in order to help and protect our children. In order to do so, we need to have more information and more skills than our own parents needed. We all want our children to grow up capable of having healthy and caring adult relationships in which sex is a part. This is a more difficult task than it used to be, and we must all work together to find ways to help our children adapt to a rapidly changing world. There are no easy answers, but the first step is to learn about what is going on today.

As James Baldwin said, "Not everything that is faced can be changed, but nothing can be changed until it is faced."

Chapter 2

From Barbie to Bratz and Beyond

Sexy Sells

What makes seven-year-old Hannah express feelings of misery about being too fat to be sexy? Could the ever-present anorexic-looking bodies of supermodels in skimpy clothing be playing a role—or the similarly clad, hugely popular, and super-skinny Bratz dolls?

How did the seven- and eight-year-old girls at Tessa's birthday party learn that it's important to be sexy so that boys will like them, and that their parents, by not buying them sexy clothes, are keeping them from being sexy and thus from being happy? One doesn't need a Ph.D. in psychology to realize that all of this is connected, at least in part, to efforts by advertisers, media producers, and the fashion industry to create a childhood peer culture that focuses on appearance and fashion.

Why does a young child like Eva hear about a blow job at school? Today no one should be surprised that in addition to all the sexualized content being directed at young children, the even more explicit sexual content in the media and popular culture supposedly directed at teens is filtering down to younger and younger children.

As we discussed in the Introduction, the problem today isn't that our kids are learning about sex. The problem is *what* they are learning, the age at which they're learning it, and who is teaching them. Children get a very powerful and damaging kind of sex education from marketers and the popular culture. They learn to want products that help them to look and act like the characters and people they see in advertising, TV programs, and music videos and on the Internet. They learn to judge themselves and others by how they look and what they can buy, not on deeper, more human and humane qualities. As parents who have other values and goals for our children, we have to compete with the power of multibillion-dollar industries.

MARKETING MANIA

Marketing to kids these days is everywhere. From the minute they get up in the morning until they go to bed at night, children are assaulted by commercial images that get firmly implanted in their brains. The goal is to turn children into shoppers for life, and marketers know a huge amount about how to do it. They know how to get children to nag their parents to buy them things. And, as you will read more in the next chapter, when we describe how children learn about gender roles and sex, marketers know that using sex and sexiness is an extremely effective way to sell products to children starting at a young age. This is the central reason why the sexualization of females permeates virtually every aspect of commercial and popular culture directed at children at younger and younger ages: Sex sells!

Take for example, the hugely successful (by industry standards, not ours) product and media line for young girls today—Bratz. There is a full line of Bratz dolls dressed in sexually revealing (or practically nonexistent) clothing, Bratz makeup and accessories, real-life Bratz clothing including bikini underpants for preschool girls, Bratz birthday party paraphernalia including a birthday cake, fast-food meals with miniature Bratz dolls, and of course, the Bratz video games, TV show, and movie.

We have heard stories about how the Bratz phenomenon is affecting young girls not just in the United States but all around the world. Parents and teachers tell us about girls who over and over again use their Bratz dolls to put on fashion shows or go on pretend dates. Here's a story that illustrates what we often hear: After dressing up her three Bratz dolls for a "fashion show," five-year-old Sasha asked her mother to put some makeup on her (lipstick, eye shadow, and nail polish), something she had begun asking for more and more in recent weeks. Then she got her teenage brother's boom box and brought it into her bedroom, put in a Britney Spears CD, and called her mother and brother to "come see the fashion show." When they arrived, they found Sasha dressed in her party dress, wearing makeup. She walked around the room wiggling her hips and holding a doll, describing to her audience what each doll was wearing, just as an announcer might do.

The next time we heard about Sasha she was very involved in playing on the Be-Bratz.com website. She got a Be-Bratz.com doll, which comes with a computer "key" that allows her to become a member of the Bratz website virtual community—part of a virtual world of shopping, fashion, and glamor. So now she doesn't even have to interact with her mother or brother as she did during her Bratz fashion show! Virtual online communities like this one are becoming more and more popular with younger and younger children. And with them has come the ability of the programmers to keep children absorbed in learning how to shop—and in the case of the Bratz website (and the Barbie.com website too), this means fixating on spending fantasy money to focus on appearance and sexiness.

In today's cultural environment, products that channel children into narrowly focused content and activities threaten to consume every aspect of their lives. For young girls, this usually means focusing on buying fashion items, looking pretty, and acting sexy. From newfangled

Barbies and sexy Bratz dolls to "old-fashioned" princess fairy tales, young girls like Sasha learn to value a certain aesthetic and a certain behavior—be pretty, be coy, and often even be saved in the end by a handsome prince. In today's popular culture, these gender stereotypes and sexualized messages are everywhere. There's hardly a medium that doesn't perpetuate these characters and these myths. On network television (and more overtly on cartoon cable channels), in theaters, in toy store aisles, in their Happy Meals, and on the Internet, children are fed these myths and these ideas. Even Saks department store recently got into the act when it introduced *Snowpeople,* a picture book for young children in which the "snowpeople" express their individuality . . . by shopping for luxury clothes at Saks. All of this exposure gives children ideas they would never think of on their own, ideas that leave them always looking for what they "need" to buy next and how they "need" to look in order to be happy.

And boys are definitely not off the hook. Marketers have put a great deal of money and talent into using violence to market products to boys. Just think about G.I. Joe, Transformers, Mighty Morphin Power Rangers, Batman, and Spiderman—with their action figures, toy weapons, video games, TV shows and movies, children's fast-food meals, birthday party products, websites, and much more. Sound familiar?

While this focus on violent themes for boys may seem far afield from the topic of this book, as you read on you'll see how the use of entertainment violence to target boys is an essential part of the picture when we think about the development of healthy relationships. The onslaught of violence makes it harder for boys to develop into caring sexual beings capable of having fulfilling and connected relationships. Boys learn harmful messages about the role of violence within relationships and in the wider community. As girls see boys' involvement with violence and boys see girls' involvement with sexiness, they all learn damaging lessons about what to value in themselves and their own gender as well as about one another.

THE POWER OF THE SCREEN

Virtually every media form studied provides ample evidence of the sexualization of women, including television, music videos, music lyrics, movies, magazines, sports media, video games, the Internet, and advertising.

—Executive Summary, *Report of the American Psychological Association Task Force on the Sexualization of Girls,* February 19, 2007

Children learn about the world and how it works, including about gender, sex, and sexuality, from what they see and hear in their own environment. Their homes, schools, and communities have always played a crucial role in providing the lessons. These days the media— ever present and ever noisy—play an increasingly important role. Marketers and the media have joined forces to use sex to sell products to children in increasingly "in your face" ways. As a result, children learn a great deal about sex and sexiness from the six and a half hours a day they spend, on average, in front of a screen. As never before in human history, a huge proportion of what children learn comes not from hands-on interactions with people and things, but from secondhand experiences with the media and popular culture. A great deal of influence and power over children's education comes not from parents or schools but rather from media producers and marketers.

The Henry J. Kaiser Family Foundation has done a series of invaluable annual reports that document the expanding role and nature of media in children's lives. The 2003 report, *Zero to Six: Electronic Media in the Lives of Infants and Toddlers,* found that 36 percent of children under age six live in households where the TV is on "always" or "most of the time." Thirty percent of children from birth to age three and 43 percent of children from ages four to six have a TV set in their bedrooms. Thus the TV becomes an essential fixture from the very beginning of their lives. Even very young children are likely to be watching TV with no adult present. Since the 2003 report came out, there has been an even bigger push to lure infants to the screen, such as the launch of a twenty-four-hour cable television channel for babies and the release of a *Sesame Beginnings* video series recommended for babies as young as three months by the generally trusted Children's Television Workshop.

A 2005 Kaiser Family Foundation Report surveyed the screen habits of third- to twelfth-graders and found they were exposed to eight and a half hours of media content each day, an increase of more than an hour a day from five years earlier. It also reported that approximately two-thirds of all eight- to eighteen-year-olds have a TV in their bedroom—and half have a video game player as well.

The Unending Barrage

During the hours children are in front of the screen, they are almost constantly bombarded with advertisements. They are exposed to an average of forty thousand ads per year on television alone—and this figure continues to rise every year. These ads, many of which contain sexualized content, give marketers an astonishing amount of access to children, often more than many parents have.

More than 80 percent of popular teen TV shows contain sexual content. Children also see abundant sexual and sexualized activity in music videos, books, films, cartoons, video games, and song lyrics aimed at teenagers (but which younger children also see). Marketers have long targeted children as potential consumers, and they know that using sex and sexiness is one of the most successful ways to get children's attention in order to make them want to shop.

The United States government has a long history of protecting children from products and practices in society that can harm them. When a 1978 Federal Trade Commission report concluded that children under age seven do not possess the cognitive ability to evaluate child-oriented television advertising (a conclusion that the American Psychological Association reiterated in 2004), Congress began to consider legislation to give the FTC more regulatory power over advertising to children. But the tide began to turn on the possibility of the FTC's playing a regulatory role when the entertainment and marketing industries launched a powerful lobbying effort in Congress against the new effort. This successful campaign not only stopped Congress from passing the new legislation, it also stripped the FTC of the limited powers it already had to oversee children's advertising.

Soon after that, another event occurred that made matters much worse. Until the mid-1980s, children's television was regulated by the Federal Communications Commission. The regulations placed limitations on marketers' access to children by specifying the number of advertising minutes allowed per hour during children's programming. The FCC interpreted this limit to mean that when a corporation developed a children's TV program with a line of toys and other products to accompany it, the whole show became a commercial and thereby violated the rule governing the number of minutes of advertising there could be per hour.

But the floodgates truly opened with the FCC's deregulation of children's television during the Reagan administration in the mid-1980s, when pressure mounted to get government to deregulate all aspects of industry. Deregulation made it possible for marketers to develop products for children directly linked to children's television programs. And the program-length commercial, a program made for the sole purpose of selling products, was born. More specifically, programs were now used to market toys to children that replicated everything they saw on the program. The first blockbuster show after deregulation was *Masters of the Universe (He-Man),* which took over the young boy culture like a storm and had the number-one-selling toys on the Toy Industry Association's "Best Selling Toys List" for quite some time. Around the same time, most of the networks that aired children's programming (there were fewer networks then than now) quickly closed their children's program production units. They no longer needed their own departments, because they could now buy their children's programming from private production companies that developed and advertised the program, toys, and other products as a package. In 1990, after intense lobbying efforts by many concerned organizations and individuals, Congress reinstated some of the FCC's regulatory power. However, reregulation failed to limit the program-length commercials and thus had limited impact on reducing the use of TV programming to market to children.

Childhood Lost

Two monumental things happened after deregulation of children's television that point the way to where we are today. First, children became a separate marketing group, with corporations treating children as consumers for the very first time. As marketers worked to create this new demographic, they became increasingly sophisticated at doing their job. Indeed, it is hard today to imagine a time when children weren't viewed as consumers and subjected to a barrage of ads and marketing campaigns. But it's important to remember that there is another model for what childhood can be, and it is a much better one, for sure.

Within a couple of years of deregulation, most bestselling toys—and an increasing number of other children's products such as branded clothing, bedsheets, and breakfast cereals—were linked to TV programs. *Masters of the Universe* and *My Little Pony* were early examples of this cross-product marketing. Very quickly TV and other forms of media cooperated in supporting one another's efforts to market to children—linking together movies, video games, and TV programs, all for the purpose of selling an increasingly elaborate array of products.

Second, and more alarmingly in terms of exposing kids to concepts beyond their ability to understand, sex and violence became primary marketing tools to capture children's attention and create voracious consumers. This meant that children's television programs quickly became much more gender-divided. Different programs, and products linked with them, were developed for boys and for girls based on the presumption that boys and girls would be interested in different kinds of products.

Initially, girls' programming focused on sweet and nice behavior and on appearance—being pretty—with shows like *Care Bears* and *My Little Pony.* But gradually and consistently, increasingly graphic sexual imagery has been used; sexiness and mean-spirited behavior crept into shows like *Powerpuff Girls,* and the sophisticated and elaborate Bratz doll phenomenon you read about earlier came on the scene. And violence became the defining feature of programming for boys, with such highly successful shows as *Masters of the Universe, Transformers, GI Joe, Teenage Mutant Ninja Turtles,* and *Mighty Morphin Power Rangers.* Each new successful program had more acts of violence and more extreme violence than the one before it.

Around this time, teachers began reporting that they were seeing more gender divisions in children's play. Girls were more involved in dramatic play themes that involved focusing on appearance. Boys were more involved in play with violent themes that were often linked to TV shows. One survey found that more than 90 percent of teachers of young children believed the Mighty Morphin Power Rangers were making the boys in their classrooms more violent.

The same 2005 Kaiser Family Foundation report mentioned earlier took a careful look at the sexual content in all types of television programming. It found that the number of shows with sexual content increased between 1998 and 2005, from 54 percent to 70 percent. But there are no data on the increases in sexual content in programming between 1984 and today, figures that undoubtedly would be much more dramatic. As jarring as these findings are, the survey did not look at the sexual content in the commercials that children see, which would have made the situation even worse. A KFF report from a year earlier found that 60 percent of parents said they were very concerned about the amount of sex their children are exposed to on TV. From talking to parents as we have been writing this book, we think the number of concerned parents is probably higher today. And parents are not concerned just about television. They are worried about the content of DVDs, video and computer games, Internet sites, and the ever-expanding field of media in children's lives.

Beyond Television

Indeed, other media, including video and computer games and the Internet, are playing a greater role in young children's lives all the time. Video game industry sales of almost $18 billion in 2007 exceeded those of the movie and toy industries. While gaming is generally thought of as being more for boys than girls, there has been a big push in recent years to expand the video game market to girls at younger and younger ages. Many video and computer games and Internet websites are now linked to dolls, movies, and TV programs popular with girls and younger children. Most simply tap into and amplify the primary themes for girls in today's popular culture—appearance, sexiness, and acting like teenagers. For example, Hasbro's *Dream Life* TV plug-in video game (recommended for children ages eight and up) allows players to enter a virtual world of teenage bliss, where they can earn "money" so they can go shopping, get their hair done, and buy fashion clothes to go to dances with fantasy boyfriends. Target actually put this video game on its list of bestselling "toys" for six- to eight-year-old girls.

The recent arrival of online virtual communities where kids engage in virtual play—whether it be Webkinz, which is gender-neutral and popular with both boys and girls, or the Be-Bratz.com website, which attracts girls like Sasha—is yet another example of the many ways electronic games and virtual communities are taking the place of the imaginative play, social interaction, and engagement that are so important for children's development as social beings. Increasingly, electronic games are the preferred activity when children get together on playdates. Handheld games often fill children's time as adults socialize with one another at restaurants, at airports waiting for planes, and for the entire length of airplane flights (except during takeoff and landing). For many children, the more they play video games, the more they need them. Other activities, which don't provide the same quick pace and "programmed" behavior, can easily seem boring.

The sexual and violent content in younger children's games is tamer than in games for older children. But young children are less sophisticated in their thinking, so less graphic material can still have a disturbing and harmful effect. What's more, as young children get bored with the games they have, they quickly look to games with content rated for older children, which means, of course, more sex and more violence.

BEYOND THE SCREEN

Sexualization in the media is just the tip of the iceberg. These sexualized messages are reinforced in many other ways as children go about their daily lives.

Toys Transformed

Go into any mass-market toy store and you will find that a large proportion of the toys on the shelves are linked to TV programs, movies, and video games. They are usually rigidly divided by gender to boot. As you walk down the aisles, you can tell just from the colors on the packages which aisles are for boys and which are for girls.

The overwhelmingly pink and pastel aisles are full of toys for girls. Almost all of these toys focus play on appearance, fashion, and sexiness. They include fashion dolls with crotch-length skirts, makeup sets, and life-size heads with wigs on which to practice hairstyles. Although Bratz has just surpassed Barbie as the bestselling doll, Barbie has long been working hard to keep at the front of the pack. Several years ago, when Mattel, Barbie's manufacturer, realized that play with Barbie dolls (and other dolls too) was ending at younger ages than in the past (a phenomenon known as "age compression" by the industry), it responded by introducing the Lingerie Barbie line for older girls— dolls wearing see-through lingerie. Brazenly, the Barbie.com website describes one new doll in the Lingerie series this way:

> The Barbie® Fashion Model Collection unveils its first-ever African-American Silkstone doll, the fifth Lingerie Barbie doll. Her enchanting ensemble begins with a delicate black merry widow bustier with pink bow accent. Her matching robe offers alluring cover. Golden hoop earrings and high heels complete this simple but elegant ensemble, perfect for dress-and-play fun!

Now Mattel has introduced My Scene Barbie, a new line of Barbies with redesigned bodies and personas that more closely resemble the Bratz dolls.*

As girls' toys focus play on fashion, appearance, and sexiness, what's happening with boys' toys? Just look for the aisles with deep primary colors and black. That's where the boys are. A majority of the toys you'll find are linked to violent media that provide scripts for how to play at being "tough guys" above all—ready to fight, and not involved in caring relationships. Each new movie has toys replicating everything seen on the screen. When the *Transformers* movie came out in the summer of 2007, we found over a hundred Transformer toys on the Toys R Us website. As boys begin to outgrow these toys, they replace them with video and computer games, also highly focused on fighting and violence.

---

*Mattel has also joined forces with the trusted *Sesame Street* program to create a Tickle Me Elmo Barbie doll, recommended for children ages three and up.

The Incredible Shrinking Dress

Now let's look at the fashion industry and its marketing efforts to turn girls into sexy objects. You can't be a parent today without noticing the revolution in the clothing being marketed to children that has taken place since you were young. Here are but a few examples of how manufacturers blur the boundaries between adults and children:

- MGA Entertainment, producer of the Bratz dolls, has licensed a line of Bratz clothing and accessories for little girls that includes a matching hip-hugger underpants and padded bra set.
- Mainstream national chains such as Target and J.C. Penney are selling padded bras and thong panties for young girls that feature cherries and slogans such as "Wink-Wink" and "Eye Candy," slang terms referring to sexual appearance and sex.
- "So Many Boys, So Little Time" is the slogan on one fitted T-shirt sold in a size made for six-year-old girls.
- A T-shirt for four-year-old girls says "Scratch and Sniff" across the chest.
- Gym shorts for ten-year-old girls have two handprints on the back—one on each cheek—zeroing in on the spot supposedly waiting to be grabbed, patted, or pinched.
- T-shirts for toddler boys carry the slogans "Pimp Squad" and "Chick Magnet."

Such products illustrate just how mainstream it has become to turn children into cute and sexy little objects and how desensitized our society has become to this sexualization of children.

The stereotypical images of sexiness used by the fashion industry to lure girls at ever younger ages into ardent consumerism also have an impact on boys. Boys often learn to relate to and value girls based on these same shallow and superficial criteria. They learn to objectify girls long before they understand sex. Some of the parents' stories in Chapter 1 illustrate how girls' desire to look sexy is ratcheted up by the reactions of boys, creating a vicious circle.

Children are also pictured in increasingly sexualized poses in mainstream advertising meant for adults. Major fashion magazines for men and women often feature photos of young children in very sexy poses, selling a whole range of products and brands that often are not just for children. One Ralph Lauren ad in *The New York Times Sunday Magazine*—surely a publication not read by the kids in the house—portrayed a girl and a boy, seemingly about eight years old. The boy closes his eyes as the girl, who has sexy long blond hair and is wearing extremely short shorts, leans in to him, holds his hand, and kisses his cheek, with apparent passion. Most of us flip right by an ad like this, increasingly desensitized to the sexualization of childhood.

Meanwhile, more and more of the products and activities marketed to little girls involve them in pursuits that used to be reserved for older girls, teenagers, or even grown women. "Play" makeup kits for young girls, always available on the toy aisles, have become a real winner (again, from the industry's point of view, not ours). Pedicure sets for seven-year-olds are a newer creation. Spa treatments for little girls are the rage in some parts of the country; girls can wear white robes just like their mothers do while having their nails and makeup done.

A recent development to sexualize girls even further is the all-in-one fashion boutiques for girls like Club Libby Lu, a chain of stores owned by Saks Fifth Avenue and rapidly appearing at shopping malls across the country. Here young girls can have makeover birthday parties that include dressing up like sexy grown-ups with clothes for the part, makeup, and fancy hairstyles. The mother of one five-year-old told us of a birthday party her daughter recently attended at an independent makeover boutique that claims to be "a special place for girls, ages 4 & up!"

First, each of the girls was made over with makeup, nail polish, hair styling, skimpy clothing, and boas. My daughter seemed a bit uncom fortable (as was I) and I think that's probably why she chose a light-colored lipstick and the less extreme clothing. Once the girls' makeovers were complete, they were shown how to pose like models for their fashion photos. Then, after the tea party, the girls were given lessons on how to strut along the "magic carpet" wiggling their hips from side to side for a fashion show. The girls focused more on choosing the right items to wear and movements to make than on interacting with each other. An overweight child seemed especially miserable throughout. What are we teaching these girls? Seeing the promotion materials for the boutique almost made me sick: *"If she can pretend, she will make it real . . . we will turn her fantasy into reality!"*

Play makeup, facials, and now makeover fashion boutiques teach little girls that they should spend their time focusing on how they look. Children learn from what they do, and when we give them toys and "special" grown-up activities to do, we're telling them this is what we value and what we want them to learn. When the activities we give them are highly structured, adult-centered activities that tell them when they play they should focus on being pretty, even sexy, we're letting the sexualized media and popular culture, not ourselves, control the lessons children will learn. And they are harmful lessons. They are very different from the ones little girls learn playing dress-up in their mother's clothes, something that can be harmless and has gone on for ages. In these activities, children play in their own childlike ways based on their own experiences and ideas. When we take this control away from them, we allow them to be pushed further down the slippery slope of sexualized childhood.

Let's hope that this fantasy doesn't become a reality! It's normal and healthy for kids to have fantasies about what they can be and become. But it's very different when the fantasies come from the children themselves and are connected to their meaningful experience than when they are molded into a one-size-fits-all template that for girls usually means focusing on being pretty and sexy. When girls play in the latter way, it often feels more like programming robots than creating rich, imaginative play.

Sexy Singers

Finally, we need to talk about the increasing role that the superstar culture of music, music videos, and reality TV plays in children's lives. Hot young stars like the Spice Girls and Britney Spears and Christina Aguilera wear very sexy clothing and dance provocatively while singing songs with very sexual and sometimes violent lyrics. These "stars" are held up for our young daughters to emulate—and for our sons to see as desirable females.

During the height of the Spice Girls' popularity, a distressed and embarrassed colleague of ours recounted the following story. While the stars and songs have changed (though at this writing, the Spice Girls are on tour again!), this grandmother's concern is similar to the concern we continue to hear about today:

> Jenna, my four-year-old granddaughter, and I were in a store buying shoes for the new school year. The radio was playing and she said to the sales clerk, "Is that the Spice Girls singing?" He shook his head no and asked if she liked the Spice Girls. She nodded her head. He asked, "What's your favorite song?" Jenna looked at him coyly and said, "Let Me Be Your Lover!" When he asked if she knew the words to the song, she began to sing the song—and to gyrate her little body. I wanted to sink into a hole and cry!

For a long time children have been exposed to popular music intended for teenagers, and often to content that parents felt wasn't appropriate. But now, in an effort to expand its reach, the music industry has turned its attention to creating edgy music for younger children. A notable example, Kidz Bop, produces highly successful albums with well-known songs sung by popular singers, with children singing the choruses. The words of some of the songs are modified for a child audience, but many remain quite "cool" and sexy. "It's hard to have a brand for kids that has absolutely no edge," according to the creator, Craig Balsam. "I really think they would be completely disinterested." The songs are marketed on TV and can be purchased from the website, and now in stores. The website has homemade-looking music videos with the songs being performed by children acting like stars. A phenomenon like Kidz Bop lures children into a world of "hot" songs and sexy behavior that can be problematic for adolescents and is definitely inappropriate for children. It takes children yet further away from the childhood they should have and need to have.

Because of the ways children think, real-life pop culture figures are likely to have a greater impact than cartoon characters or toys such as the Bratz dolls. When Britney Spears was at the height of her popularity, teachers and parents reported that girls as young as four were obsessed with her and acted out her sexy moves and songs at home and at school. A few years ago, Diane was on a *Good Morning America* segment about the sexualization of childhood. The reporter first showed girls and then boys about six to eight years old a video clip of a scantily clad Britney singing one of her songs with accompanying sexy body movements. As the video played, the girls viewing her began to wiggle and move like Britney, and some even mouthed the words of the song. The reporter asked the children why Britney was moving the way she was. They responded with, "The boys like her to move that way," and "That's how to be sexy." One child commented about her clothes by saying, "She wears a little shirt like that because it's sexy." The children's parents, who were viewing the children through a one-way mirror, voiced shock and concern that their daughters knew the movements and the song. They seemed to have little idea that their children were so knowledgeable about Britney. Unfortunately, they might not be as surprised by such behavior today!

So far, we've described sexiness as a marketing tool aimed directly at younger children. It's important to realize that the sexualized content in our culture designed for tweens, teens, and grown-ups—the media, billboards, window displays at shopping malls with seminude mannequins, racy Internet websites, and the like—also reaches younger children on a daily basis. Disney's phenomenally successful *High School Musical* movies are a case in point. Ostensibly the movies are for older kids—teenagers—but we know almost no eight-year-old girls who don't know and love them. And the movies have found their way into every imaginable marketing venue, and some unimaginable ones!

According to one survey, about 40 percent of Internet users aged ten to seventeen said they had seen online pornography in the past year. Of those, 66 percent said they did not want to view the images and had not sought them out. They happened upon the sexually explicit websites while surfing the Internet. The figure for such unwanted exposure has gone up from 26 percent in 1999–2000.

Of course, what we're talking about isn't a matter of being prudish or moralistic. There's an emotional health issue at stake when children view pornography. They are exposed to content well beyond their ability to comprehend. If a picture is worth a thousand words, one can imagine the damage done to kids who see pornography. Pornography objectifies people (especially women) and takes sex out of the context of even the pretense of a caring relationship. It is difficult for children to unlearn these attitudes.

NEVER TOO YOUNG TO BE A CONSUMER

Children are especially vulnerable to marketers' efforts because of the very way they think. Under the age of eight, they have trouble understanding that the purpose of an ad is to get them to buy something. If they see a child smiling and looking happy, they don't realize it's because the child is being paid to look that way. Young children believe what they see, so that when sexy behavior or appearance is connected to happiness, they believe it will be like that for them too. Children are especially vulnerable to sexual and violent content because they are drawn to the dramatic images, even if those images are scary or confusing.

Marketers know about young children's vulnerabilities, and they exploit them. They work very hard to create a strong childhood culture that divides children from adults. They deliberately create peer pressure to attract children to products that their parents don't want them to have, products that are generally not good for them and sometimes can be extremely harmful.

A Lion in Lamb's Clothing

A few years ago, in response to sagging sales, the Disney Company launched a huge new line of products with the Disney Princess theme—a conglomeration of all the well-known sexy princesses from its popular animated movies. The marketing of Disney Princesses to little girls has become a resounding success to the tune of $4 billion in sales in 2007 for dolls, pretend cell phones, lunch boxes and backpacks, sheets, clothing, books, video games, DVDs . . . the list would fill up the next few pages.

Little girls have always indulged in princess fantasies, and many parents don't see the inherent harm in letting their little girls indulge them today. But playing princess was never the way it is with Disney Princesses. The overwhelming message the Princesses convey is to look pretty, aka sexy, so they can hook their prince. Everything else is secondary. And we have heard of more and more little girls who dream of being princesses when they grow up.

What surprises us most is that the role the Disney Princess phenomenon plays in the childhood culture of young girls seems to be off the radar screen in most discussions about the sexualization of childhood. Indeed, we feel that Disney movies and the princesses featured in them provide one of the first avenues for luring young girls into the sexualized materialistic world. Along the continuum of sexualization, the Disney Princess collection of toys and other Princess products definitely falls closer to the more wholesome end. However, the Disney Princesses tend to enter the lives of girls earlier than many of the other sexy products. And the Disney Princess product developers do slip in some sexier fashion items—for instance, the "Glamorous Jasmine Peignoir," a ruffled, low-cut nightgown that is available in sizes XXS and up and, according to the product description, "will have your little princess shimmering at her royal slumber parties."

Less overt, but no less troubling, is the fact that very young girls take on the roles of Disney Princesses in their play—imitating the scripts and images they see in movies, DVDs, and videogames and on TV and computer screens. The concerned mother of four-year-old Jenny told us about a puppet show created by her daughter. Jenny began the show by placing prince and princess finger puppets on her index fingers. She told her mother that the princess was Sleeping Beauty and the prince needed to rescue her because the "mean mother" hurt her. The prince finger puppet came up to the princess puppet and as they hugged (index fingers wrapped around each other) Jenny said, "The prince will save the princess. Then he'll kiss her," she said, and puckered her lips. Her mother tried to expand the play beyond this frequently acted out rescue plot by suggesting, "How about this time something different happens?" Jenny scrunched her eyebrows together doubtfully and asked, "Like what?" To the mother's distress, her reply to Jenny, "How about this time the princess saves the prince?" led to Jenny heatedly screeching, "Oh, no! The prince HAS to rescue the princess. He loves her! She's pretty so he wants to marry her!"

This scenario is similar to many stories we've heard about the play of young girls who are caught up with Disney Princesses. Through acting out stories like this over and over again, girls are primed from very young ages to focus more and more on prettiness, sexiness, and being desirable to boys. And they use these experiences to build their identity as females. Once girls are on this conveyor belt, they're pushed to move along on it toward increasing sexualization.

We recently heard about one little girl who exclaimed that she is going to have a Disney Princess wedding when she grows up. She may actually be able to do this, because Disney has now introduced real Disney Princess weddings that can be bought by grown women!

Certainly, Disney Princesses and movies are not the only media-product line to contain stereotypical and sexualized content for the youngest children. However, the degree to which most adults trust Disney and the extent to which the Princess products are flying off the shelves warrants our special attention.

The Bottom Line

All these sexual images and products are not intended to sell children on sex—they are intended to sell them on shopping. As Cynthia Peters, a regular commentator for ZMag.com, said in an insightful ZNet piece, "Teach seven-year-olds that sexual expression is a matter of accessorizing and you've secured a lifetime of purchases in the lingerie department. Disassociate sex from non-market feelings (pleasure, desire, intimacy) and associate it instead with consumable superficialities, and you'll not only keep the rabble in line, you'll have them lined up at the mall."

Now you understand the nature of the beast—namely, what and how the contemporary commercial culture contributes to the everyday experiences you are having with your children as well as to the experiences we described in Chapter 1. The essential next step in the journey of preparing yourself to meet your children's needs is to learn how and why children are so deeply harmed by this sexualized culture. You will need this lens before we can talk about how to protect children and help them grow up to become caring and fulfilled adults.

Chapter 3

Sexual Development Derailed

The Toll on Children

In order to devise strategies that promote age-appropriate sexual development for children and adolescents and counteract the harm caused by inappropriate sexual messages, caring adults need to first understand how sexual development occurs. It is also important to recognize how sexual development is affected by children's experiences, as well as understand what is normal at certain ages and what is not. This chapter will give you a crash course. You will find more detailed information in the resources recommended at the end of the book.

From a very early age, and in increasingly sophisticated ways at each new stage, children work hard to figure out the confusing messages about gender, sex, and sexuality that surround them. They strive to learn about their own bodies and to understand what it means to be a female and a male. They want and need to learn how to negotiate intimate relationships, how to love and be loved, and, as they get older, how to have sex as part of a caring relationship.

KARA'S STORY

This story provides a small window into how age-appropriate sexual development occurs when children are growing up in an environment that supports it.

Four-year-old Kara loved going to the wedding of her parents' friends Mary and Hannah. Mary and Hannah, who live in Massachusetts, where lesbian and gay marriages recently became legal, already have a three-year-old daughter, who was a flower girl at the wedding. Now Kara talks about it with everyone and plays "wedding" all the time with her best friend, five-year-old Liza. She sometimes has her own little sister, Brit, play the role of flower girl.

One day, Kara's father was taken by surprise when Kara reported to him that when she grew up, she was going to marry Liza, and then added, "But of course, we'll have to have two weddings!" He asked her why they would need two weddings. Kara responded: "Because you get to have a baby when you get married! And if we're two girls that get married, we'll both want to have a baby. So we'll have to have two weddings!" Then she added, "But if I marry a boy, then I'll only need one wedding!" Wisely, Kara's dad did not begin correcting her. He just said, "Oh, I'm glad you told me what you think will happen."

Kara's "solution" illustrates the incremental, unique, and often charming but inaccurate ways that children arrive at an understanding of their world. Kara's age-appropriate thinking is quite different from that of the adults around her. It's more like a slide show than a movie; she doesn't make logical causal connections, but focuses on one aspect of a situation at a time and relates what she sees only to herself. It's the visible and concrete aspects of what she observes that matter, not what lies beneath the surface. She doesn't notice the inconsistency in her thinking—she thinks that she and Liza will need two weddings to have their two babies, but she doesn't wonder why Mary and Hannah have only one marriage and one baby! Throughout, she doesn't know that her logic is faulty.

Adults know that the conclusion she has reached—that weddings automatically produce babies—is clearly wrong, but it's not wrong to Kara. Having the "right" information about where babies come from isn't as important at her age as being taught that ideally having babies is connected to a caring relationship and that weddings symbolize caring relationships. Over time, with the help of an accepting and thoughtful adult, Kara's understanding will evolve into a more accurate view of sex and reproduction.

It's hard to predict exactly what any individual child will learn from what she sees and hears, because no two children interpret the same experience in quite the same way. A strong, connected relationship with an adult with whom a child feels safe sharing her thinking is essential for healthy sexual development to occur. But for now, Kara is happy with the conclusion she has reached, and it serves her well.

In today's climate, many children aren't as lucky as Kara. They don't have parents who are able to talk with their children about sex and sexuality with the understanding and support Kara's father provides. Or worse, their parents discourage them from talking about sexual issues at all. They live in a society in which schools are not able, for political reasons, to provide age-appropriate sex education. As a result, much of what they learn about sex and about relationships comes from the popular culture that surrounds them. When they see female pop stars dressed in highly sexualized ways (that look like hookers to us), when they discover at age seven that boys judge girls by how skinny and "sexy" they are and that girls who want to be popular need shirts that expose their belly buttons, they are learning very narrow and stereotyped ideas about how to be a male and a female person. They learn that females should spend their time and energy on their appearance, which leads many girls to make shopping and primping their major extracurricular activities. In this environment, children need supportive adults more than ever to help them interpret what they see and learn alternative ways to see themselves and the world.

MAKING SENSE OF CHILDREN'S
SEXUAL DEVELOPMENT

Understanding children's sexual development is not always easy, because it is usually so different from how adults think. But it is an essential first step in preparing yourself to help your children process
today's sexualized environment. It provides a lens for understanding
what is going wrong today, the harmful messages children are learning,
and what you can do about it. What follows here is a list of key characteristics related to sexual development in children:

- *Sexual development begins at a very early age and involves much
  more than just learning about the birds and the bees.* Interest in issues such as body parts and how they work and where babies come
  from and how they are made is an important part of early sexual
  development, but it is only a start.

- *Children use the information their environment provides to build
  their ideas about sex and sex-related issues.* This is clearly happening
  with Kara. She drew many conclusions from her experience of
  going to a wedding. She learned something important about
  friendship and relationships—that ideally you marry the person
  who is your best friend, someone you have a good relationship with
  and care a lot about.

- *Children's ideas about sex and sexuality develop gradually.* The
  process begins during infancy as babies explore their bodies, learn
  about body parts, and experience the pleasures of physical contact
  and affection that can come from cuddles and kisses. At around
  the age of eighteen months they learn the labels "boy" and "girl"
  and which one applies to them. They then begin to figure out what
  these labels mean. What they learn is influenced by many factors,
  such as their age, the thinking that goes with their level of devel-

54

opment, and the experiences and information their environment provides—what their families do, as well as the media they see and the toys they play with.

- *Children use what they already know to interpret new experiences.* Kara's story reveals that she already knows a lot about sexual development. She knows that, at least in her world, weddings occur between two people who really like each other. She knows that it's females, not males, who have babies. She also has learned to associate the concrete event of marriage with having babies, which shows an awareness of social conventions in our culture. And she has ideas about the origins of babies that she is quite confident about—the actual act of getting married. The only problem with this last lesson is that she got it very wrong, another characteristic of children's thinking.

- *As children build ideas about gender, sex, and sexuality, they don't always get it "right."* With more experience, however, they get new information that helps them revise their thinking and arrive at increasingly sophisticated and accurate understandings. It is the fact that new ideas grow out of what came before that makes caring adults worry so much about the foundation that is being laid for so many of today's young children.

- *Sexual development does not occur in isolation; it is connected to other lessons children are learning at the same time about themselves, others, and how to function in their world.* The ideas children develop about themselves as separate, competent people and as males and females (beyond the anatomical information) affect their ideas about sexuality and sex. Their ideas are also deeply linked to what they believe about the nature of relationships and how care and affection are expressed in relationships.

- *Children learn in their own individual and unique ways, but what they learn generally falls within the parameters of their age and level of thinking.* When a child has a new experience, as Kara does when she attends the wedding, she uses what she already knows to figure it out. In the process, she builds new (although sometimes incorrect) ideas about how she understands the relationship among marriage, weddings, and babies. What she concludes is probably unique to her; no other child is likely to come up with quite the same conclusion from the same experience. Yet given how she thinks, the meaning she has derived makes sense to her. With different earlier experiences or at a different age and stage, she probably wouldn't have reached the same conclusion that she did here.

- *The lens an adult uses for looking at and understanding sexual issues is very different from the lens a child uses.* Often when children say things that seem connected to sex and sexuality, they have very different meanings for the children than they have for adults. For instance, when Kara says that when a woman gets married she gets a baby, she isn't necessarily thinking about the actual sexual process that creates the baby, though adults can't help but bring that idea into their thinking. When young Jason in Chapter 1 said he wanted to have sex with Ashley, he too had a very different (and incorrect) concept in mind than the adults in his life had. It would not have been very helpful to Kara if her father had tried to explain—even in simple terms—his fully formed adult understanding of where babies come from and their relationship to weddings and marriage. Kara's comment shows she is focused on the fact that when two people have a loving relationship and get married babies follow, not specifically how the babies get there (here again, slide show versus movie thinking). Similarly, when a child wears sexy clothing, an adult may immediately make the association with sexuality, but the child is only making a statement about what she has learned about how to be pretty.

The more we adults are able to look through the lens children are using, the better we will be at understanding what they are learning, how they are affected by the sexualized culture, and what to do to promote their healthy development. Knowing how children learn and understanding the basics of early childhood development will help you figure out how to respond to their efforts to make sense of their world. This knowledge can help you understand what they might be learning about sex and sexuality from the current popular culture and why the lessons can be so harmful. It can also help you develop age-appropriate strategies for dealing with these destructive messages. If children are given information that matches their level of development and ability to understand, they are more likely to develop a healthy appreciation of sexuality and to be able to counteract the negative messages they are receiving. If they are given information that is confusing or upsetting, they run the risk of learning lessons about sex and related issues that undermine healthy sexual and gender development and that can also undermine and damage their ability to have successful intimate adult relationships when they grow up.

HOW YOUNG CHILDREN THINK

Parents are often surprised when their young children, up to about age seven or eight, come up with unique, often delightful, but sometimes worrisome comments about their experiences. It's often hard to realize that such comments provide a powerful window into how children are using their current level of thinking to interpret their world. In part, children learn what they do from the sexualized popular culture, and sexual development occurs as it does, because of how young children think. Looking at children through a developmental lens makes Kara's response and the responses of other children described in this book, as well as the responses of your own children, so much more understandable. It can also help you figure out the most positive and constructive ways to respond so that your children will learn the lessons you want them to learn.

Understanding how children think and learn can arm you with the information you need to resist becoming desensitized and thus be able to make informed decisions for your children.

- *Young children are drawn to information that is visible and concrete, unfamiliar, dramatic, or even scary.* This helps explain why they are so easily seduced by violent actions and sexy physical appearance (large breasts, scanty clothing), as well as actual sexy behavior (flirtations, struts, embraces). It also helps explain why marketers use dramatic images, including sexy and violent ones, to capture children's attention in order to sell them things.

  This kind of thinking is at work in James's drawing of a "professional wrestling girl with big boobies" (undoubtedly a description he learned from someone older than himself) when he focuses on dramatic big red lips and big breasts. As with many children, James uses art to show what is most important or puzzling or scary to him. The drawing becomes a vehicle for making contact with his teacher; at the age of five, it would no doubt be harder for him to raise the issue with her through words alone. We see a similar process at work when Hannah talks in the bathtub about Isabelle's appearance and equates her thinness with "sexiness." Much of the current sexualized media and advertising, with their shallow focus on appearance, as seen in the recent deluge of "makeover" shows, for example, feed into and reinforce this one-dimensional concrete thinking.

  Because children tend to focus on the most dramatic and salient aspects of how things look, they are especially susceptible to the sexual images that surround them. Big breasts on view, scantily clad bodies, and sexy body movements are not part of the everyday life experiences of most children. That's why they grab a child's attention when they do occur. The more dramatic and extreme the images, the more likely they are to attract the child. The desire to capture children's attention in order to turn them into consumers at an early age helps explain some of the increasingly extreme portrayals of sexual characteristics that are to be seen in popular culture these days. For example, one study found that the size of the muscles of action figures linked to violent media, such as *Teenage Mutant Ninja Turtles* and professional wrestling, got bigger and bigger every year, and scantily clad female professional wrestling action figures that caused concern ten years ago seemed very tame compared to one available five years later named "Sable," an action figure with a whip whose huge breasts spilled out of her bra top.

- *Young children's thinking tends to focus only on what they can see. They don't look at what lies beneath the surface of objects, images, and actions—such as the motives, intentions, and feelings underlying sexual behavior.* This way of thinking makes children especially vulnerable to focusing on the overt aspects of being male and female and of sexuality, without understanding what the underlying relationships and emotions mean. When Eva asks her mother about blow jobs, she is probably focused on the physical act of a blow job, not on what her mother might say about the nature of the relationship between partners that could lead to this sexual act. Children can't understand the underlying feelings that can lead partners to want to have sex. This is one reason why they think about sex differently from the ways in which healthy adults think and, to some extent, why it's so hard to talk to children about sex.

- *Young children tend to focus on one thing at a time, not on multiple aspects of a situation and the relationships between those aspects.* As Hannah cries in the bathtub, she focuses on one thing—how "fat" her body looks compared to Isabelle's body. She is also focusing on one thing when she decides that it is Isabelle's thinness alone that makes her so popular. She doesn't look at other factors that might contribute to Isabelle's popularity. She considers only the one thing that is most obvious to her—Isabelle's appearance. This kind of thinking predisposes young children to think that how they look (not what they do and think) determines what people think of them and how they are treated. Sadly enough, this is often true in our culture. Indeed, it seems that many people in our society have a case of arrested development when it comes to thinking about appearance. At age seven, Hannah has concluded, from her experience and current level of thinking, that being thin is equated with being sexy and that being sexy is equated with popularity. Strongly influenced by the sexualized messages of her culture, she has begun to build a one-dimensional connection between dieting and thinness, popularity and sexiness. Many other young girls in this culture are reaching similar conclusions, as witnessed by the fact that girls are going on diets and showing up at eating disorder clinics at younger ages than ever before. And it only gets worse with age; we have begun hearing about middle school girls purging their lunch in school toilets every day!

- *Young children's causal thinking is more like a slide show than a movie because they generally focus on one thing at a time.* They tend to deal with one static moment or a series of static moments that they don't see as logically connected. They are generally not yet able to focus on logical causality, relationships between events, or how a transformation occurs from one event to another. Kara provides a great example of where such thinking can lead. She puts each piece of her marriage scenario together separately without making a "movie" of how babies manage to magically appear after a wedding! This naturally limits children's ability to understand why people exhibiting sexy behavior are acting the way they are.

- *Young children's thinking tends to be egocentric—that is, they often relate what they see to what it has to do with themselves.* (For many people, this doesn't change as much as it should, but it is supposed to!) When his teacher asks James what he knows about wrestling girls, he responds with one egocentric piece of information: "I saw it on TV with my big brother." He says nothing about *what* he saw. When Kara goes to the wedding, she egocentrically relates it to what it means for her. Egocentrism can help explain children's frequent failure to consider the impact of their actions on others. Perhaps this is also why the children we discussed in Chapter 1 seem, for the most part, to be so unself-conscious about the sexual issues they are raising. When Bratz doll lover Sasha (in Chapter 2) uses sexy gyrations and puckered lips during the fashion show she puts on for her mother and older brother, she is probably totally oblivious to what her behavior might signify to them.

• *Young children can't fully distinguish between what is pretend and what is real.* When they see an advertisement featuring a male ogling a female in sexy clothing, children will probably not consider or understand that both parties are being paid a lot of money to look and act this way. Because their thinking is more like a slide show than a movie, they aren't able to follow fully how transformations occur—how something gets from one state to another—such as when two people aren't in love and then are in love, how a woman goes from not being pregnant with a flat stomach to being pregnant with a bulging stomach, or exactly how someone goes from being fat to being thin. Joanne Cantor, in her book *"Mommy, I'm Scared": How TV and Movies Frighten Children and What We Can Do to Protect Them*, illustrates this using the case of many superheroes who transform from one state into another, such as Superman, the Hulk, and the Power Rangers. According to Dr. Cantor, young children do not understand these transformations and are therefore often terrified by them.

As children grow, their thinking processes gradually become more adult. We see the beginnings of this transition when seven-year-old Hannah realizes that what one eats contributes to how much one weighs. She has begun to create a "movie" (to make a logical causal connection) that focuses on something she cannot completely see (what happens to the body when one eats or doesn't eat).

EXPLOITING HOW CHILDREN THINK FOR PROFIT

Media and marketers spend a lot of money on psychological research. They know how children think and they use this knowledge to reel children in, to encourage them to buy into the sexualized culture of consumerism. Unfortunately, most parents know much less about child psychology than the marketers do. Even worse, because the industry's messages have become so normalized in our culture and because knowledge of the thought processes and emotional and psychological needs of children has been so obscured, many adults have become desensitized to the full impact of these messages on children.

This desensitization is an important part of what is going on today. It reduces many parents' ability to think about the sexual content that surrounds their children from their children's point of view. It leads some parents to make unwise decisions for their children. It helps explain why some parents allow highly sexualized figures such as Britney Spears, Bratz dolls, and professional wrestling into the lives of even very young children. It also helps explain why some parents manage to resist the most graphic sexualized products but then rationalize buying a sexy but less extreme product because it seems better by comparison.

This situation helps explain, at least in part, the popularity of the Disney Princesses and, more recently, the *High School Musical* movies, which are linked to other media, dozens of products, and much media hype. As with the Disney Princesses, these movies focus more on appearance and sexiness than they do on sex. As one father said to us, "My ten-year-old daughter is absolutely enthralled with the *High School Musical* movies. And it's a great relief. Both are so much tamer than what her friends are usually obsessing about." However, these movies lead children down the same path toward sexualization as do more overtly sexual teen movies.

Why Does It Matter?

Eileen Zurbriggen, the chair of the American Psychological Association's Task Force on the Sexualization of Girls, aptly reports, "The consequences of the sexualization of girls in media today are very real and are likely to be a negative influence on girls' healthy development. We have ample evidence to conclude that sexualization has negative effects in a variety of domains, including cognitive functioning, physical and mental health, and healthy sexual development." And while the task force report concludes that very little research has been done on how young girls are affected, it argues that there are grounds for serious concern.

Again, the problem is not that children are learning about sex. The problem is that the sexualized childhood is harming young children at the time when the foundations for later sexual behavior and relationships are being laid. Children are exposed to information about sex and sexiness that they can't understand but that can confuse and worry them, and can also influence the ideas they develop and their behavior. They are forced to deal with sexual issues when they are too young, when the way they think leaves them vulnerable to soaking up the messages that surround them with few resources to resist.

Girls learn to judge themselves and others based on how they look; in essence they learn to see themselves as objects. And boys learn to judge them this way as well. The resulting objectification undermines their ability to have connected, caring relationships, which will, in turn, harm their ability to have caring relationships in which sex is a part when they grow up.

REMOTE CONTROL CHILDHOOD

In addition to encouraging precocious sexuality, the media's sexualization of childhood contributes to an interconnected set of other disturbing and far-reaching problems. Although these problems may not at first seem to be related to the sexualization of childhood, they are. Understanding them and the connection they have to the way your children learn about sex, sexuality, and relationships will help you approach every problem your child encounters in a holistic way rather than as a series of separate issues, each needing separate attention.

A recent scene at an airport—which one of us witnessed while waiting for a delayed flight—is telling. Several children from different families, both girls and boys between the ages of about three and ten, were waiting nearby. All of them were "well behaved." All but one, including the three-year-old, were focused on some sort of screen, engaged in a handheld or laptop electronic activity such as playing video games or viewing a DVD with headphones. A closer look at each screen made it easy to tell whether a boy or girl was playing. The boys were engaged with games centered on sports and fighting, while a Disney Princess handheld game and a Dora the Explorer DVD entertained the girls. The one child who was not connected to a device, a girl about six years old, was quietly walking around with her dad, looking out the window at a plane pulling up to a gate, watching the jetway connect with the plane door. As she saw the luggage being unloaded from the plane onto a conveyer belt, she asked if this is what would happen to the suitcases they had checked.

While all the children were certainly well behaved, the difference between the activities of the child interacting with her father and the plugged-in children was startling. Only one child was out in the world, observing and exploring it, figuring out how things work. As she found interesting things to observe and learn, she shared her excitement with a caring grown-up. As she watched the suitcases being unloaded, she asked questions that revealed she was beginning to draw connections (make a movie in her head) about what would happen to her own suitcase on the plane. She wasn't depending on a preprogrammed object to control her and keep her busy. She was *disconnected* from electronics, but wonderfully *connected* to her environment and to her father.

In contrast, plugged-in children are having secondhand experiences rather than direct involvement with the real world. They also are engaging in a process that is being controlled by someone else's "program." The only decision they have to make is which screen to use and when to turn it on. Any child who chooses the same game will do similar things. And being good at it means doing exactly what every other child who is good at it does. The children using the devices could be doing exactly the same thing anywhere—at home, at a relative or friend's house, at a restaurant, or in a car. This difference between the two kinds of airport activities—those programmed by the screen and those programmed by the child—isn't just academic. It's central to understanding who today's children have become owing to the "electronic culture" and how parents can help them resist the impact of that culture.

Children are spending increasing amounts of time in front of a screen, both at home and when they go out into the world. The screens involve them in an agenda not of their own making. Someone else (the creator of what is on the screen) is in control of what children see, what they think about, and even what they learn. Even many of the popular toys children use when they're not involved with a screen, such as Star Wars, Batman, and Transformer toys, are highly structured and take control away from children. On the other hand, open-ended toys, such as play dough and blocks, allow children themselves to be in control because these toys can be used in an endless variety of ways, depending on the interests, skills, and creativity of the child.

Children of today are living a remote control childhood, a childhood in which many of their activities are controlled by outsiders—corporations, marketers, and the media—who, as discussed in Chapter 2, are interested in children only as potential consumers. It doesn't really matter what specific electronic activity children are engaged in; all such activities change the whole *process* children use to interact with their world. Sasha's staging her sexy Bratz fashion shows is a perfect example of remote control childhood in action. In a sense, when she is performing with her dolls in the fashion show, it is as though she is following a scripted program about what to do with them—dressing them up in sexy, prepackaged, and prescriptive store-bought clothes and moving them around in sexy ways. Sasha engages in very little of the rich and imaginative play that helps children work on their own needs and gain a sense of inner confidence and power.

As children like Sasha follow the program provided by the TV show producer or video game or toy designer, they're not figuring out how things work or coming up with ideas of their own through creative and imaginative play and problem solving. Indeed, it often seems as if they are being programmed like robots. These children are especially affected by the harmful messages we've been describing, both because so many of the programs contain sex and violence and because children haven't developed the skills necessary to analyze and resist them. Understanding the problems remote controlled childhood can create will help you help your children learn to appropriately and effectively use those aspects of media that can have positive benefits while reducing the risk of their becoming robots. We help you do this in Chapter 5.

Problem-Solving Deficit Disorder

While programmed activities often look really exciting in the ad or on the toy box, children usually quickly become bored once they engage in them. Once they figure out the program, there's not much else to do. If your children often say they're bored even though they have a room full of toys, this may be what's going on with them. These programmed activities have very limited ability to change or grow as the child does.

However, even though your children may quickly become bored, the more they use these remote controlled items, the more they "need" them. If children's ability to come up with their own ideas is undermined or never develops in the first place, they don't have the necessary resources to create their own activities. They don't encounter interesting problems to solve. Do your children often run to the TV set or the video game player when they have free time because they "have nothing to do"? Are they dependent on having a programmed activity? Could this be considered an addiction? This may well be the case for some children.

Many children who are having remote control childhoods suffer these two seemingly contradictory experiences—boredom in the midst of plenty, and increasing dependence on being plugged in. The resulting condition can be called "problem-solving deficit disorder," or PSDD. One preschool teacher told us,

> I used to put out interesting materials and the children would be excited trying to figure out what they could do with them. Kids might watch what others did, but most came up with their own ideas of what to try. Now when I put the same materials out, the children ask, "What do they do?" It really makes me sad. And often, when kids do actually start playing with the material, things quickly fall apart as children get into conflicts about sharing materials that they don't seem to know how to solve.

When children see themselves as problem finders and problem solvers, they develop curiosity about their world and confidence in their ability to figure things out for themselves. They see the world through a lens that says "I can do it" and "I want to do it." They develop unique interests and skills, not quite like the skills of any other child. They are better equipped to think for themselves and to figure out creative solutions to real problems.

Most relevant to the discussion here, being good problem solvers enables children to resist the pull of today's programmed world and its destructive messages. It empowers them to resist obsessions with fashion and appearance, with sexy looks and sexy behavior. It helps them develop alternative and broader interests, ideas, and behaviors.

Remember Tessa and her friends at her birthday party sleepover? They were convinced that getting their mothers to buy them shirts that exposed their belly buttons would bring the sexiness, popularity, and happiness they so desperately desired. Given how these little girls are being programmed, they may be right. But even if they succeed in getting what they want, their happiness will probably only last for a few minutes—or hours—or days before the novelty wears off and they find the next item that promises to bring them fulfillment. Of course, the girls are problem solving—but it is a problem of the popular culture's making, not their own. To successfully solve it by getting the tops they lust for, the girls develop problem-solving skills such as how to nag, manipulate, and guilt-trip their parents into buying them what they want!

The First Addiction

Remote control childhood serves the interests of corporations and marketers very well. What better way to create consumers for life than by teaching children to want more and more at younger and younger ages? To get satisfaction from *getting* rather than *doing*? Instead of being encouraged to work on their own internal needs and get satisfaction from what they actually accomplish, children learn to associate happiness and a sense of well-being with getting the material things they want. This process of equating acquiring objects with happiness could be considered a child's first drug. As with any addiction, when children get the item they crave, it gives them a real high—a quick fix. But it is generally a superficial and short-lived fix—one that quickly wears off—while the children are prevented from working on the qualities they need to develop within themselves. Here's what getting a quick fix looks like through the eyes of one mother:

> My son recently had his sixth birthday party. He was very excited about his presents. The first thing he did after the party was sit down for at least a half hour looking at all the presents—mostly toys. One by one he took a toy box, examined all the other toys in the toy line that were on the box, and pointed to the picture of the toy he wanted next. Then he turned on the TV. Maybe he was tired from the party. But as he turned the TV on, I thought, "Oh my God, he's more interested in choosing the next toy he wants than in playing with any of his new toys!"

Children are learning the push-button, quick-fix approach to life. Instead of developing the inner resources and skills that lead to long-term happiness and success, they too often focus on buying just the right thing at the right time to achieve fleeting happiness, popularity, instant success, and sexiness. Over time, they run the risk of depending more and more on their quick fixes to find happiness, while losing out on the longer-lasting satisfaction and sense of well-being that come from hard work and from using one's creativity and imagination. No wonder so many children seem powerless to resist the sexy messages assaulting them at every turn.

Age Compression

"Age compression" is a term used by media professionals and marketers to describe how children at ever younger ages are doing what older children used to do. The media, the toys, the behavior, the clothing once seen as appropriate for teens are now firmly ensconced in the lives of tweens and are rapidly encroaching on and influencing the lives of younger children. In addition, there is a blurring of boundaries between children and adults, as demonstrated by the similarities in clothing marketed to both groups by the fashion industry. Age compression is especially disturbing when it involves sexual behavior. Children become involved in and learn about sexual issues and behavior that they do not yet have the intellectual or emotional ability to understand and that can confuse and harm them.

Compassion Deficit Disorder

From birth, children gradually learn how to relate to and have compassion for others from the experiences they have in their own relationships, as well as from their observations of how other people treat one another in life, in books, and on the screen. These experiences teach children how to connect with others in order to get their own needs met. They also teach children how to meet the needs of others—either in positive ways that promote caring, connection, and cooperation, or in negative ways that promote self-interest, disconnection, and objectification of the other person.

It is deeply troubling that society is providing the optimal conditions for raising a generation of children who are at risk of developing compassion deficit disorder. Today's children are learning many negative ways to relate to one another. In the media and popular culture, children endlessly see that sex and sexiness, not affection, are the primary focus of relationships between adults. They see that it's normal to treat oneself and others as objects and to judge people by what they buy and how they look. Over and over again they see aggression and violence as the preferred way for people to solve their conflicts. Acquiring an object to "hook up" with for sex for the night becomes the be-all and end-all—though "the object" quickly becomes boring and is thrown away.

PARENTS AS PROBLEM SOLVERS

By now, it will be amply clear to you that there is a big problem. But the problem is not that children are learning about sex when they are young. The problem is *what* today's sexualized environment is teaching children. The problem is that they are learning the *wrong* lessons. They are learning lessons about sex and sexuality, self-image and their bodies, and the nature of relationships that make it harder for parents to parent and teachers to teach. Children are learning lessons from today's sexualized environment that can undermine the very foundation they need in order to grow up to be capable of having caring relationships of any kind, including those relationships in which sex plays a vital role. And now that you understand the problem, you are much better equipped to be the creative and effective problem solver you will need to be to support the positive, holistic development of your child in today's sexualized childhood.

Chapter 4

The Toll on Parents,
Families, and Schools

DIANE'S STORY: IGNORANCE IS BLISS—OR IS IT?

A few years ago, I was invited to give the keynote address at a large regional conference for parents and parent educators on children's health and safety. I was asked to talk about how today's violent and sexualized media and commercial culture can undermine children's health, development, and ability to play. I enthusiastically accepted the invitation, welcoming the opportunity to give parents the knowledge they need to combat the hazards media and marketing create for their children.

A week after the invitation was issued, it was suddenly withdrawn. One of the major corporate sponsors of the conference, a large toy manufacturer (some of whose products had previously been criticized in my work), asked the conference organizers to disinvite me.

Question: Why might the toy industry want to suppress what I have to say about media culture and play?

Answer: Giving parents the child development information they need in order to understand how the commercial culture causes harm and how to deal with it is bad for big business. It's more profitable when parents are in the dark about what's going on. Of course, one could argue that this is how it's supposed to be. A corporation's job is not to promote the well-being of children, but rather to maximize profits for its shareholders. It's up to parents to protect their children, right? That's certainly what we hear all the time from the corporations and the media: "Don't blame us. It's parents who are to blame."

PARENTS AND FAMILIES FEEL THE HEAT

By now you've seen a lot of what is going on in the commercial culture that contributes to the sexualization of childhood. You've already read about how this affects children's daily lives and why it's so bad for them. Now it's time to assess and appreciate how and why it is so hard for you to do your job as a parent these days.

The Nag Factor

Is nagging an issue in your home? Do you find that your children often treat you as if their very happiness and self-esteem depend on whether you say yes or no to their demands? Do you often feel frustrated that no matter how you resolve one issue regarding buying or not buying some item your child covets, the next struggle pops up all too soon?

At the same time that the toy industry tries to silence critics and prevent them from providing parents and other caring adults with the information they need to do a better job, it also does a great deal to make the task of being a good parent harder. For example, in September 2001, the Campaign for a Commercial-Free Childhood (CCFC) held a summit in New York City to protest the "Golden Marble Awards." These awards were given for the so-called "best"—almost exclusively defined as most profitable—advertising and promotional campaigns directed at children as part of a two-day conference sponsored by Brunico communications on "breakthrough marketing to kids."

In response, the CCFC presented the "Have You Lost Your Marbles Awards" to companies that employed marketing practices deemed most harmful to children. The *Most Harm to Families Award* was given to the advertising agency that did research on how to encourage children to nag their parents to buy the products advertised. The headline on the ad company's press release proclaimed, "The Fine Art of Whining: Why Nagging Is a Kid's Best Friend." The copy below said, "The Newest Nag Factor Study Reveals 21 to 40 Percent of Sales of Jeans, Burgers and Other Products Occur Because a Child Asked for It." The complete report gave marketers the information they needed to take full advantage of the Nag Factor in their marketing campaigns—all at the expense of the adults who care for the children.

Clash of Cultures

Imagine the scene that Sandra, the mother of twelve-year-old Alyssa, recently described:

> Last week I took my daughter Alyssa shopping for a dress for her first junior high school dance. We started out with such happy anticipation. But I couldn't believe the dresses I had to veto because of the length (almost up to her crotch) or the neckline (a lot of cleavage), the completely missing backs, or the clinginess—or sometimes all of the above. We both got more and more tense. Finally Alyssa burst into tears and lashed out at me, "You're so mean! Drew and Bryn choose their own dresses! I just won't go to the dance. Forget it." And she stormed out of the store. I felt like I was caught in a vise. I wasn't going to let her out of the house looking like a hooker. But I hated that setting this limit damaged our relationship. Then when we got home, my husband said I was too prudish, that Alyssa would look great in a sexy dress, and I felt like it was my turn to scream. Why is it so hard to do what I know is right?

Here's Alyssa's account of the situation:

> I just can't take it anymore. My mom thinks I should wear what she
> wore when she was my age. But how long ago was that? If Mom only
> knew the things that really go on, she'd hit the roof. I'm old enough to
> decide for myself what I wear. All my friends do. What's wrong with
> looking sexy? Even my father gets mad at Mom for being so uptight.
> Drew said she'll lend me a dress and I can go to the dance from her
> house. I'd die if I had to wear the kind of dress my mom wants.

Alyssa and Sandra's conflict is an example of the clash of cultures
that many parents and children experience all the time. Parents tell us
that battles like this about appropriate clothing and shoes happen now
with children as young as five. The sexual images and behavior that
children see in the media create a great divide between the messages
of the popular culture and the messages most parents want their children to receive.

It is not only children who pay a high price for the sexualization of
childhood—you, the parents and other caring adults, do too. In a 2002
survey of parents of five- to seventeen-year-olds, almost half reported
that their biggest challenge was trying to protect their children from
the negative societal influences in the outside world. The report concluded that parents feel that society "barrages youngsters with harmful
messages . . . these hazards are a source of constant worry, posing an
even tougher problem than household finances or lack of family time
for many parents." While low-income and single parents were more
likely to include financial pressures on their list of serious concerns, a
majority of them still listed protecting their children from negative societal influences as their biggest challenge.

The survey also looked at how parents thought they were doing at
teaching their children the lessons parents feel are most important.
Forty-nine percent did not feel they were succeeding at teaching self-
control and self-discipline. And 42 percent had concerns about mate-

rialism; they reported feeling they had not succeeded at teaching their children to save money and spend it carefully. Many parents said that their children were concerned about "brand names" and that the concern increased with age.

Because of the clash of cultures, children sometimes seem to have two disconnected boxes in their heads. One is filled with the attitudes, values, and behaviors you try to teach—the family culture box. The other is filled with lessons learned from the sexualized media and popular culture—the commercial culture box. Often the values in the two boxes are at odds with one another. It's hard for children to connect the two boxes. So they go back and forth between them, depending on the demands of the current situation. Not surprisingly, conflicts occur when you're operating from the family culture box and your children are operating from the commercial culture box.

Certainly, the media and popular culture have had a powerful influence on the children described in this survey. Being a "good" parent today means fighting the prevailing culture at every turn, with ever younger children. This conflict was apparent in Connie's sex education class when the boys who saw pornography on the Internet argued that sex can be just for fun and doesn't need to be within the context of a relationship. These messages come straight from the commercial culture box. These aren't the attitudes most parents want their ten-year-old sons to have about sex. Most parents would want the family culture box to contain the lessons Connie is trying to teach that connect sex with a caring relationship. A similar clash of cultures is at work in Alyssa's battles with her mother over wearing the sexy dress of her choice to the dance. As Alyssa stands firmly in the commercial culture box, Sandra, from her position in the family culture box, believes that girls should never be sex objects, most certainly not at the tender age of twelve.

Children today are constantly being yanked back and forth between the two boxes, often having to choose between the world out there and you. It's an unfair situation for them and for you. The more rigid the boundaries between the boxes, the greater the strain and alienation.

One effective way to reduce tension is to build links between the boxes—to stay close and connected through conversations and empathy. Figuring out how to do this is not easy. You'll find the help you need in later chapters.

Premature Adolescent Rebellion

The current climate is also creating what we call "premature adolescent rebellion." Many very young children today rebel against their parents long before adolescence. Instead of seeking advice and support from their parents, children turn to their peers for guidance through the thickets of sexuality, consumerism, and sexualization.

Parents see their children drawn into the sexual maelstrom and find themselves struggling to figure out what to do. One mother from the survey reported, "Probably the biggest mistake we ever made was purchasing him a TV. I didn't do it, his godmother did. But I foolishly condoned it and let it come into his room. . . . My son just went crazy. I think it was the music videos he started watching . . . among other things, the female dancers were virtually naked. They were vulgar. They moved vulgar, talked vulgar. He thought it was okay and started talking vulgar too."

What if this mother had banned this treasured gift from her son's bedroom as Sandra banned Alyssa's coveted sexy dance dress? In easier times this would be the sensible thing to do. Today it could lead to a war in the family and alienation between mother and child. Ultimately, it could even lead to a premature adolescent rebellion such as the one Alyssa has when she storms out of the store fuming at her mother and then plots to borrow a sexy dress from her friend. A premature adolescent rebellion is brewing with even younger children at Tessa's sleepover birthday party as she and her friends discuss how to manipulate their parents into buying them sexy clothes.

The alienation of children from their parents created by premature adolescent rebellions makes it much harder to be a good parent. It drives a wedge in parent-child relationships at a time when adult guidance is most needed. This is just the way marketers want it! It's the reason that marketers study how to capitalize on the Nag Factor. It's also why advertising and media work so hard to create a culture in which adults are generally portrayed as invisible, stupid, or obstructionist, depriving their kids of what they want. Children who see their parents as standing in the way of obtaining the happiness or popularity promised by an ad become angry and resentful. This paves the way for nagging and plotting to influence parental buying decisions, all in the service of corporate greed.

The Culture of Fear

Keeping children safe is the number one priority of virtually all parents. Day in and day out, we are reminded of the many physical and psychological dangers that threaten our children's safety. There is so much to worry about—child molesters, kidnappers, guns, junk food, tainted food, lead paint on toys, harmful messages about sex and violence in the media. The culture of fear makes it difficult for parents to let children work on the age-appropriate activities and actions they need to do on their own in order to become autonomous and responsible.

As children get older, the sexualized commercial culture adds even more worries to parents' already lengthy lists. It's just not fair! Struggles over appearance and sexy behavior in girls and aggression and bullying in boys strain relationships. How are parents affected by having to be so vigilant, to raise children in a "culture of fear"? One grandmother captures the dilemma rather well:

> My heart often aches for my son and daughter-in-law who are trying to do a good job raising their six- and eight-year-olds today. Already at six, their daughter has friends who wear clothes and act in ways that embarrass me. The eight-year-old often comes home from school in tears because someone has said or done something mean to her. Both girls hate riding on the school bus because the "big kids" (the fourth- to sixth-

graders) do things like tease each other about being girlfriends and boyfriends. And after school, the parents are afraid to let them play outside because they're worried it isn't safe.

So they've ended up buying the girls clothes that make me and even them feel uncomfortable, they're constantly going to school to talk to the teacher and principal about how the older one is being treated, they drive the kids to school and pick them up, which makes them late for work, and they keep the girls indoors watching TV and DVDs or playing on the computer after school—and you can guess what they end up seeing! One thing after another creeps into my grandchildren's lives, bit by bit. My son and daughter-in-law seem to lurch from one crisis to another. It just keeps getting harder and harder and I really worry about where it's going to lead.

Raising children in a society where you're constantly worried about the physical and psychological dangers that can befall them harms both your relationship with your children and your ability to parent well. Despite your best efforts, it's next to impossible to feel as if you're being a good enough parent, let alone a good parent! Understanding the challenges you're having with your children and why you're having them lights the way for you to find the right solutions for the specific problems in your family.

WHY CAN'T PARENTS JUST SAY NO?

Diane was on a national television program recently, arguing that government should be doing more to protect children from harmful marketing practices. The person she was debating dismissed this possibility, claiming, "If parents would just say no, there wouldn't be a problem. They're the grown-ups. They should take charge and show their children they're the boss." This is the most common response you'll hear in discussions about who is responsible for the problems raised in this book, although it usually comes from people who haven't been around children much lately.

Let's follow the argument of the "Just say no" approach. Wouldn't the world of childhood be a better place if Sasha's mother just knew how to say no to the Bratz dolls and all the other Bratz products and media that are contributing to her daughter's premature interest in sex and sexiness? Why do Sasha's parents fuel her obsession with the Bratz marketing empire by letting so much of it into their home? The Bratz dolls' influence on young girls would just go away if parents like Sasha's didn't buy them, if they just said no. Right?

Wrong! Even if parents said no all the time, there still would be a big problem. Big business makes sure there is absolutely no way parents can fully hold back the floodgates on their own. In the words of one very frustrated parent, "You can't say no to everything! Even when you do say no, much of what you say no to slips into your child's life anyway—at a friend's house or as a birthday gift from a friend or relative. This was true when my child was four and it's even truer now that she's fourteen! And it's not good for anybody when parents and children treat each other like enemies all the time."

It's time to stop blaming parents for the sexualization of childhood. While knowing how to say no the right way is an essential parenting skill, no amount of saying no can offset the harm that today's sexualization is having on children and families. Everyone who cares about children needs to work to replace this empty slogan with education and action that will make a difference. Here is a summary of arguments you can use to support your efforts to do so.

TWELVE REASONS WHY JUST SAYING NO ISN'T ENOUGH

1. "Just say no" is a simplistic response to a very complex issue that requires complex solutions.

2. It doesn't solve the problem. Children will be exposed to some of the harmful influences anyway—at homes of friends and relatives and at school, in shopping malls, and in movie theaters.

3. It doesn't help children understand what they are exposed to in the popular culture. Children need a way to make sense of their experiences.

4. It can cut parents off from helping their children process what they do end up seeing and from having some influence on what they are learning. This can lead to the media and marketers having an even greater impact.

5. It doesn't help children learn to be responsible people who can make responsible choices even within an all-pervasive sexualized popular culture.

6. Children end up feeling guilty when they see or get things that they know their parents disapprove of.

7. Parents end up feeling guilty and inadequate when they're told again and again that it's their job to say no to the popular culture but they can't possibly fully succeed.

8. The stage is set for premature adolescent rebellion as children are often forced to choose between their parents and their friends.

9. It puts unfair blame and a disproportionate burden on parents to solve a societal problem.

10. It lets the media and marketing industries completely off the hook.

11. It allows politicians (most of whom are beholden to the industries) to avoid their responsibility to create policies and regulations that protect children.

12. It can be an exhausting process for both parents and children.

The entire society has a responsibility to help parents do their job well, rather than to thwart their efforts at every turn. However, even though that's not the case today, there are many powerful and effective things you and your family can do that focus much more on getting to "yes" with your children than always ending up at "no." The next two chapters describe these positive steps. Chapter 8 offers guidelines for parents of adolescents. And the final chapter discusses what's needed to create a society that would better support your efforts to raise children who have healthy relationships with their bodies, their sexuality, with you, and ultimately with their partners.

SCHOOLS FEEL THE HEAT TOO

Parents recount many concerns about the information and stories of a sexual nature that their children bring home from school. This makes sense, given that the issues discussed so far don't just magically disappear when children go through the schoolhouse door. Issues of sex and sexual behavior have always come up with high school students. But now teachers and school administrators of elementary and preschool children report that they are dealing with the consequences of the sexualization of childhood on a regular basis. Of course, some of these stories make their way home.

Zero tolerance policies, which require the suspension or expulsion of students who exhibit any violent or sexual behavior, are being enforced with greater frequency for sexual incidents with younger children. As is so often the case, when children do what makes perfect sense to them, given what they have been exposed to, they end up getting punished. Many adults today are so hypervigilant that they punish children even when the so-called infraction is harmless. For instance, you've already read about the boy who was almost suspended from kindergarten for telling a girl he wanted to "have sex" with her when all he really wanted was to give her a kiss because he liked her. And *The Washington Post* reported that in 2007 Maryland suspended 166 elementary school children for sexual harassment, including three preschoolers, sixteen kindergartners, and twenty-two first graders.

More and more schools are implementing official dress codes because of the increasingly explicit clothing so many children wear. Dress codes once used only in high schools and then in middle schools are now being considered in elementary schools. As one teacher said, "What can we do about school-age children with short skirts, low-cut tops with skinny straps or no straps at all, high heels, makeup, jewelry, training bras, thongs showing with low-cut jeans?"

An experienced health counselor for the schools in a wealthy suburban community reports that middle school officials have had to cancel school dances because of sexual activity such as lap and sandwich dancing, where a girl dances between two boys who press up against her in front and in back. They are also having problems at dances these days with "freaking," a kind of dancing in which a boy and girl grind against each other in a simulation of sexual intercourse. And now the problems are spreading even to elementary schools. The same counselor recounted one instance where an elementary school principal contacted her for help when he got word that a group of fifth-grade girls were trying to pressure boys into kissing them and doing bump-and-grind dancing. School officials are having to rethink how and when sex education is dealt with in the elementary schools.

Teachers' Stories

Teachers of kindergarten and preschool children report that they too are dealing with the effects of sexualization on a regular basis. They see an impact on social relationships and the way children interact both within their own gender group and between genders.

One teacher of three- and four-year-olds told us,

There are so many ways I see sexual issues coming up in my classroom (even though I know it's not directly related to sex for the children). Several girls have expressed their desire to be "sexy" when they play dress-up. Sometimes it almost seems like they want to see how I

83

react to it. I have asked them what "sexy" means. One girl said it means "pretty." Another said it means "kissing and stuff." A boy once pointed to a girl and said, "She looks very sexy today." She was wearing wedge-heeled shoes and a short skirt and had on nail polish. I have overheard kids saying to each other, "Are you his girlfriend [or her boyfriend]?" In the dramatic play area, some boys and girls play boyfriend and girlfriend and put their arms around each other in hugs. A couple of times they've even tried kissing. They say they're playing "teenagers"!

When children feel safe, they bring up things they're concerned or puzzled about—in their play and with trusted adults. That may be why this teacher feels that the children are looking for a reaction from her when they use words like "sexy." It's likely that if they've used the word before, they've gotten a response that indicated this was not a "regular" word. So they may now want to see what the trusted teacher does. This makes how she responds especially important. In an environment where children feel safe, it also makes perfect sense that they might kiss and hug each other and play at being a girlfriend or a boyfriend, if they are being exposed to this in the outside world and are trying to fig-ure out what it means. Young children use their pretend play, a vital part of any good preschool program, to work out experiences, espe-cially those experiences that are dramatic, puzzling, or scary. Finally, given that boys learn from the commercial culture at a very early age to judge girls by how they look and what they wear, we shouldn't be sur-prised that sexualized clothes and shoes that are being marketed for young children make it into preschool settings—even at age four!

Carrie, a kindergarten–first grade teacher, related this story:

It was the first day of school. I brought my class to the cafeteria for lunch. The children were assigned seats at one of six round tables. I sat down next to a five-year-old girl. "That's the popular table," she said matter-of-factly as she gestured over her shoulder to one of the other ta-bles. I was taken aback, but followed her finger to see where she was pointing. I looked back at her and asked, "Popular? What do you mean by that?" "Oh, you know, they have the nice clothes," she explained. I thought about that for a moment, and since it was the first day she'd ever been in school, I asked, "Where did you learn about that?" Without a moment's hesitation she answered, "The Disney Channel!"

This kindergartner shows she has learned very well what the Disney Channel, with its recent emphasis on sexualized tween girls, teaches. Others judge you, and you judge others, by how you look and what you can buy. If a family can't afford to buy the right things, or if it tries to bring some reason, rather than fashion, to its kindergartners' wardrobes, then there are winners and losers. And everyone knows which is which.

Another first-grade teacher reported that her boys seemed to have split personalities:

> I'll say things have changed! I have six-year-olds (mostly boys) reacting to words in stories that can have a sexual connotation—"suck," "gay," "pump," and "blow," and the name "Dick"—with a giggle, gesture, or gasp. Sometimes it seems as if the boys have split personalities. In a one-on-one situation with me or another child, they can be very sweet. Then as soon as they get together they act rowdy and mean like tough little bullies—with each other and with girls.

These boys, at age six, are already bringing sexual language into the classroom. Even though they do not fully understand what the words mean, they do this in a way that shows they think there's something "silly" or embarrassing or upsetting to adults about them. In doing so, they may be asking for the adults' help in figuring this out, or they may have learned that it's a way to get a dramatic response or a way to act like a "big kid." Whatever the reasons, what they are learning will gradually influence their attitudes toward sex.

But the teacher's description of the boys' "mean boy–nice boy" behavior is often a lot more distressing than the language they use. It shows these boys are already deeply enmeshed in the clash of cultures and have two separate boxes in their heads—the commercial culture box that's telling them to be tough, macho bullies, and the family culture box with its more humane, loving, and connected behavior.

This kindergarten–first grade teacher described the impact of sexualization on her class:

I teach a combined kindergarten and first grade at a small urban K–8 school. My public school is diverse both socioeconomically and racially. I've been teaching for eighteen years, but this past school year was one of the most challenging I've ever experienced. The social dynamics were a constant source of stress and strife for everyone, including the children's families. At the end of a particularly frustrating day I described the situation to my principal this way: "We have two 'middle schools' in our school this year. The middle school, and my K–1!" And boy, did my children feel like middle schoolers.

That is how the year felt. The problems I encountered, mostly around the oversexualization of my students, caught me off guard and utterly unprepared. I had five-year-old girls vying for the attention of the "coolest" first-grade boy. They would push to be near him at the sand table, and cheer if I did and groan if I didn't place them in his book group. Students in the class referred to each other as "boyfriend" and "girlfriend." I've always had a music time when the children can dance to children's songs and we play games like "freeze dance" [the children freeze when the music stops]. This year, music time had a new dimension as students danced out the social scenarios they had seen in music videos of popular rap singers. My five-, six-, and seven-year-olds talked about "being in the club" and "drinking Heineken." I got reports of my kindergarten girls getting into "catfights" (that was the word the kids used) before or after school, mostly over one of the boys. They wrote about the music world in their daily journals and turned the block area into a radio station. Sometimes they used the hollow blocks to build a stage to perform on. Small cylindrical blocks were their microphones. This type of play was okay with me, except for the gyrations they made when they sang and the mean-spiritedness—who was "in" and who was "out"; that was a constant battle.

Another aspect of this that negatively impacted our classroom community was the idea of certain kids wearing the "right" sneakers. While it only involved some of the boys, the rest of the class was affected. We had class meetings about it, but it was a continuous struggle. One morning, a kindergarten boy and a first-grade boy got in a physical fight (pushing down, hitting) when the younger boy said he was wearing "Carmello Anthonys" and the older boy said, "No, those are Jordans." Another boy, whose mom refused to buy expensive sneakers, had repeated meltdowns (crying, throwing things, yelling) when other boys arrived at school with a new pair of sneakers, a stylish shirt or outfit, or big plastic gold rings.

This is a particularly worrisome example of what can happen in a kindergarten classroom today, but we often hear stories like this. The sexualized childhood environment influences dramatically the social climate in the classroom. It teaches children to treat one another as objects—being judged and treated based on what they can buy and how they look. They are having their feelings hurt and getting into conflicts if they aren't wearing stylish clothes or don't have the right label on their sneakers. Issues that used to be the domain of much older children are now defining relationships between girls, between boys, and between girls and boys who are five and six years old. And as we discussed in Chapter 3, this kind of early objectification of self and others becomes a part of objectified sexual relationships as children get older.

That boys are so focused on the brand names on shoes illustrates the harmful lessons children are learning about what to value in themselves and others. That the boys actually come to blows over the brand names means they are learning to use the violence modeled for them in the pop culture in their own disputes. The emotional stress on the boy whose mother remains firm about not giving in to the brand-name pressures shows what a double-edged sword rigid limits can be. Children's academic learning is also affected, such as when the children's reading group behavior depends on whether the class heartthrob is in a particular group or not! The bottom line is that this experienced teacher is being forced to alter how she teaches and works with children in order to meet the children's needs in this new cultural environment.

This teacher, like so many others interviewed for this book, admits she feels ill prepared to deal with this new world. She would like to pretend it doesn't exist, but she realizes it's vital to try to understand and respond to children who bring in content related to what they buy and wear and how their bodies look, including looking sexy. Children need help working out what they're being exposed to, and teachers can play an important role in this process. Without this help, children's academic and social and emotional development can suffer, as much of their energy goes into dealing with the stresses and strains caused by their efforts to understand the sexualized and commercialized world that surrounds them. Teachers are the only adults in most children's lives who have been specially trained to understand and promote their development and learning. That said, it is often asking too much to consider teachers as a line of defense against the harmful effects of our commercial and sexualized culture—they already have overly demanding jobs!

PARENTS AND TEACHERS AS PARTNERS

The sexualized cultural environment is making the jobs of both parents and teachers infinitely more difficult. But rarely do parents and teachers talk to one another about what's going on, unless a situation really gets upsetting or out of hand. There are several reasons why:

- There's not much of a tradition, especially in the United States, of parents and teachers working with one another on sexual issues.
- With young children, before things get very explicit and the connections with overt sexual behavior become more obvious, parents and teachers worry that they're reading too much into the children's behavior. They don't want to be viewed as alarmist.
- In spite of all the graphic sexual messages in our popular culture, most adults not only don't feel very comfortable talking to children about sexual issues, they have a hard time talking about these issues with one another. This may be partly a result of the almost complete lack of meaningful or relevant sex education in American schools, today and in the past.
- There's a tendency for teachers to blame parents for what's happening with their children and for parents to blame schools for allowing such behavior.
- Most teachers and parents aren't quite sure what an appropriate response to the behavior is, so they don't see the point of having a conversation. Teachers especially might worry that the conversation would make them seem ill prepared or ignorant, or that they would say the wrong thing.

Certainly, everyone who cares about the well-being of children needs to learn more about how to help children deal with the sexualization of childhood. But as it becomes clear where much of the responsibility really lies, it is easier for parents and teachers to stop blaming themselves, one another, and the children and to focus on doing everything they can to work *with*, not against, one another to counteract the impact of these harmful and degrading messages.

Chapter 5

Helping Children Through the Minefields

What Parents, Families, and Schools Can Do

Now that you understand more about the nature of the problem and how it affects children, it's time to look at constructive ways to counteract the sexualization of childhood and promote positive development. While we can't promise that the suggestions that follow will answer all of your questions and solve every problem, we do promise that you can make things a lot better for your children (and yourself). The goal is to help you develop a way of being with your children that will make it easier for them to navigate the sexualized minefields of our culture. This will help them become adults capable of healthy and loving sexual relationships. The eleven guidelines suggest strategies to help you get started. Many of them are also designed to help you get beyond "just saying no."

But this is by no means an exhaustive list. The guidelines are not mutually exclusive, and working on one guideline will often also connect with others. You will no doubt have your own ideas about how to implement the guidelines as you go along. In Chapter 6 we provide examples of parents and teachers who have put these strategies into practice. These examples bring our recommendations to life and demonstrate the ways informed adults can make a huge difference in how the sexualization of childhood affects children.

GETTING DOWN TO BASICS:
GUIDELINES FOR PARENTS

1. *Protect children as much as possible from exposure to sexual imagery and related content in the media and popular culture.*

The more sexualized imagery children see, the more confused and even scared they can become, the more time and energy they spend trying to process material that is beyond them, and the more harmful lessons they learn. For example, this is what happened with James after he watched a professional wrestling program on TV with his older brother. Think of yourself as keeping your finger in a hole in the dike: Try to keep the water (sexual content) out as much as you can, but realize that some will get in anyway.

Fortunately, there are many ways to limit exposure to inappropriate messages in the media without creating a "war" in the family. The younger children are, the more control parents have. As your children get older, you can help them learn to be selective about what they watch. A less direct but essential approach is helping your children find enjoyable activities other than just sitting in front of the television or playing video games. Of course, you must know what's going on in the media in order to know what to allow and what to limit (see the next guideline).

It's also important to understand the various rating systems for media and toys and how they can help you make decisions (in spite of their limitations). The movie rating system, the one that is best known, works as a general guide, but it has definitely fallen victim to age compression. Movies that would have been considered acceptable only for older children in the past are now often approved for younger children.

Less well known are the rating systems for TV shows and video games. Toys are generally rated based only on age, not content, and often, except for the statements like "not suitable for children under age 2 because of small parts," the age rating is whatever a manufacturer chooses it to be.

In all rating systems, outside, impartial experts are rarely involved, and there is little public information as to how the ratings are determined. In addition, the systems are not coordinated with one another. A movie rated for PG-13 audiences might have a spin-off video game rated for Everyone or Everyone 10+, as well as toys linked to the movie recommended for children three years old and up. So the rating systems are a starting point, but more homework is needed.

WHAT YOU CAN DO
To Limit Exposure to Sexual Content in Media and Popular Culture

Television and other electronic media are the most frequent sources of children's exposure to sexualized popular culture. Getting these forms of media under control is one of the best ways to reduce exposure. You and your child can work together on the following issues.

• *Use media rating systems to help you decide what media are and are not okay.* Here is a guide that summarizes them for you:

A CRASH COURSE ON MEDIA RATING SYSTEMS

TV Ratings

TVY	**All Children.** Including children ages 2 to 6.
TVY7	**Directed at Older Children.** Ages 7 and above.
TVY7-FV	**Directed at Older Children.** Contains fantasy violence.
TVG	**General Audience.** Deemed suitable for all ages.
TVPG	**Parental Guidance Suggested.** Because of intense

violence (V), sexual situation (S), strong coarse language (L), or intensely suggestive dialogue (D).

TV14   **Parents Strongly Cautioned.** Contains content deemed unsuitable for children under age 14. Contains strong V, S, L, and/or D.

TVMA   **Mature Audience Only.** Designed for adults and not suitable for children under age 17. Contains strongest V, S, L, and/or D.

Video, Computer, and Internet Game Ratings

EC   **Early Childhood.** Suitable for children ages 3 and older.

E   **Everyone.** Content suitable for ages 6 and older. May contain minimal violence and/or infrequent mild language use (i.e., suggestive and profane).

E10+   **Everyone 10+.** Has content that may be suitable for ages 10 and older. May contain mild violence, mild language, and mildly suggestive themes.

T   **Teen.** Content may be suitable for ages 13 and older. May contain violence, suggestive themes, crude humor, blood, simulated gambling, and occasional strong language

M   **Mature.** Content may be suitable for ages 17 and older.

AO   **Adults Only.** Content that is suitable only for persons 18 years and older. May include intense violence and graphic sexual content and nudity.

Movie Ratings

G   **General Audiences.** All ages admitted.

PG   **Parental Guidance Suggested.** Some material may not be suitable for younger children.

PG-13	**Parents Strongly Cautioned.** Some material may be inappropriate for children under 13.
R	**Restricted.** People under 17 require accompanying parent or adult guardian.
NC-17	**No One 17 and Under Admitted.**

• *Decide how much "screen time" is okay.* "Screen time" equals the total time spent in front of any kind of screen (television, computer, video game, etc.). Setting limits together on screen time reduces the overall amount of time your children (and you) spend being deluged with information over which they have little control; this often reduces the stress on the family. Once you've decided together what the limit will be, there's much less arguing.

• *Work with your children to develop rules and routines about their TV watching and media use.* With your children's involvement, draw up definite plans of *what* will be watched, and *when*. Knowing what and when they can have screen time—say, an hour a day after dinner to watch agreed-upon shows or play agreed-upon video games—reduces the time and energy that needs to be spent figuring out what is and isn't okay every time children have free time. It leaves time for them to develop other interests and skills. It can reduce the stress on everyone of constantly having to decide what is and isn't okay, because it has already been decided. It helps children learn to take responsibility for their own screen time. With younger children, you can make the media schedule into a chart of "___[child's name]___'s SCREEN TIME." If you use simple drawings representing times of day and particular shows, your child can learn to "read" the chart.

The rules and routines you establish are more likely to work when children feel they have a voice (but not complete control) in the decisions that are made, because the rules then become theirs too. The regular negotiations and adjustments to the rules that occur with age and as new issues arise will help children learn to think through the issues involved in making good media decisions. We think that working out rules and routines together is far preferable to the common approach of using screen time as a reward and taking it away as a punishment. Working out rules teaches children how to take responsibility for their media decisions, a vital skill for children growing up in today's world, whereas the adult imposing rewards and punishments does not.

• *Plan what to do when the TV and other media are turned off.* Many children experience "PTVT" (Post-TV Trauma) when they turn the TV or video game system off and have to figure out what to do next. Turning off the screen involves leaving the fast pace of a world someone else has created and having to reconnect to one's own resources—a hard transition for many children. You can make this transition much easier for them by thinking of a range of simple things they can do to get over the PTVT—like setting the table for dinner, asking you or another family member to read them a book for a few minutes, or getting crayons and paper from a convenient location.

Many children also have a hard time figuring out what to do when they have free time and are not involved with media. The more you can help your child develop a range of meaningful interests and activities, both with you and alone, the easier it will be for them to resist the lure of media.

2. Learn about the media and popular culture in your child's life—popular TV programs, movies, video and computer games, fashion, celebrities.

A lot of parents (and teachers) find this hard to do because the content isn't what they would choose to pay attention to and can be disturbing. Often new shows slip into a child's viewing repertoire without parents' knowing much about them. Once there, it's more difficult to get rid of a show if you discover it is offensive. Being aware of new media sooner rather than later will help you make more informed decisions about what you believe is suitable for your child. Having this information will enable you to talk with your children in meaningful ways about what interests them and what they have seen. And it will make it easier to work out "rules" and other solutions for problematic issues that come up.

WHAT YOU CAN DO
To Keep Up with Children's Media and Popular Culture

- *Collect information from the children themselves.* Talk to your kids about the media in their lives—TV shows, music, video games, websites—and what they like and don't like about them. Ask about what their friends really like.

- *Make sure you look at the most popular items, at least a couple of times, so you are able to talk with your children about them.* If something has already been approved by you, look at it (as with video games or toys) or watch it (as with television programs or movies) with your children and ask them to explain things you have questions about. If you are unsure about the suitability for your child, look at it on your own. If necessary, record TV shows and movies for later viewing when your child is not around. (Recording shows is a good idea for another reason: Your kids can watch them later on, and you—or they—can fast-forward through the commercials so that the viewing time is shorter and you avoid the ads.)

- *When making decisions about what you will let your kids see, use descriptions, reviews, and ratings available on the Internet and elsewhere.* See the Resources section at the end of this book.

• *Learn from and share what you know with the parents of your children's friends.* Ask other parents to tell you what aspects of media and popular culture their children see, and to describe to you what they know and think about them. In addition to helping you learn from other parents' experiences, this is a powerful way to find parents who are willing and able to share your concerns and work on solutions together.

• *Remember that, beyond media, it's also important to keep up with the real-life experiences related to sex and sexiness, violence, and commercialism that children have in the home, at school, and with friends.* This is necessary homework in order for you to be able to connect with your children around what they're dealing with. It's good for conversation if they see you as interested and aware, rather than as out-of-it "old fogies."

When your children mention some new fad, ask them about it and then try to find out more on your own. The Internet is often very helpful with this. If there is a popular new TV show, record it so you know what it's about and can talk about it. We realize that sometimes you will be exposed to things that you would never be involved with if you weren't a parent, and you may resent having to spend your time this way. But remember, it contributes to your effectiveness as a parent—and it is a burden that will end as your child grows up.

3. Get beyond the "Just say no" approach.

Protecting children from the onslaught does not mean that you should "just say no" to everything that might expose them to inappropriate sexual content. If you are too rigid as a parent, children will begin at early ages to sneak behind your back and be afraid to tell you about whatever disturbing images and messages they do encounter. You will be cut off from being able to talk to your children about what they are seeing, and you'll have a hard time influencing what they are learning. Of course, this does not mean that you never set limits.

WHAT YOU CAN DO
To Get Beyond Just Saying No

- *When possible, try working out solutions with your children.* Children better understand and are more invested in solutions they have helped to create, and they will be more inclined to cooperate and stick to the solutions you devise if they feel that their voices matter. Mutual decisions, even when they involve limits, are more tolerable for children and more effective for all of you. This process also contributes to a crucial goal of all good parenting: to help children gradually develop more self-control and thoughtfulness.

- *When you do need to set limits or say no, try to do it in a constructive way rather than a punitive way (that is, by using your power over children to get your way).* Say something like, "I know you saw that show at Jared's house, and we've talked about how much you want to watch it here. But I've watched it too, and it just makes me too uncomfortable to let all the —— (whatever seemed inappropriate) into our house. But I'm glad we talked about it."

4. Establish safe channels for talking about sexual development and related issues with children, starting when they are very young.

Children need to know that trusted adults are there to help clear up confusion and answer their questions about what they see and hear (no matter how uncomfortable their questions might make you!). When children are young, this usually doesn't mean specific questions about sex—but over time it will. In Chapter 1, Hannah, who tells her mother how she's feeling about her body, and Eva, who asks her mother about blow jobs, are two children who feel safe turning to adults to help them deal with their concerns. If and when children do have questions about sex or need your help in dealing with sex-related issues, they are more likely to raise them with you if you have helped them feel safe from early on. The bottom line is that for children to thrive sexually and every other way, they must feel that it's safe to ask you questions and bring up concerns.

WHAT YOU CAN DO
To Establish Safe Channels of Communication with Children

• *Let children know it's okay to raise any and all issues with you, including sexual issues.* Many children know more than their parents think they do. Too many adults act as if a problem won't exist if it isn't acknowledged. This attitude makes children think that the adults in their lives do not want to or cannot help them with their questions and problems. Some children even worry about being punished if they raise issues that they think they're not supposed to know about. The more comfortable children feel raising sexual and other loaded issues with you when they're young, the better able they will be to rely on adults to help them process the more complex concerns they will have as they get older. As children grow up, safe connections with adults become even more important. The next chapter illustrates what can happen when parents and children build strong connections, and demonstrates the power that comes from working closely with children right from the start. Simply telling children "It's okay to talk about anything you want" probably won't work. Nor will asking a direct question like "Have you heard anything about sex you want to talk about?"

The best way to begin is by making give-and-take conversations a regular part of family life, as described in the next guideline. In the context of such discussions, you can occasionally make comments like "I wonder why she dressed like that? What do you think?" or "I didn't like it when he did that. Why do you think he did it? Do you have any ideas about what else he could have done?" Such questions help break the ice and convey to children that it's okay to talk about it if they want, without putting them on the spot.

• *As you talk to your children, keep in mind that having the "right" answers and responses is less important than getting used to talking about, and sharing information about, these issues.* Sometimes you will give new information to extend your child's understanding. Other times, you will need to clear up misconceptions. You won't always know exactly the right thing to say—and your children won't always say what you hoped they would, either! Don't feel you've done irreparable damage if you say something you later wish you hadn't. The simple process of talking and sharing ideas—and in so doing, maintaining a connection with your kids—is what is most valuable.

5. Make age-appropriate give-and-take conversations about sexualization of childhood issues an essential part of your relationship with your child.

Creating and maintaining channels of open communication when children are young paves the way for their feeling comfortable talking with you about whatever sexual information they come across. These conversations present opportunities for you to learn what's going on with your child, and to provide reassurance, clear up misconceptions, and influence what she learns. The more you can work issues through with your children, however difficult these issues may seem, the more influence you will have on your child's healthy development.

WHAT YOU CAN DO
To Have Meaningful Conversations
with Children About Sexual Issues

• *Don't blame children or make them feel guilty or ashamed when they do or say something that seems inappropriate.* Too often children are blamed and punished when they say or do something that reflects the sexually charged world they live in today.

- *Take your child's point of view and see the world through his or her eyes.* This can really help you figure out what led to the "inappropriate" behavior and decide how you will respond.

- *When talking to children about sexual issues, take your lead from what they do and say.* A big goal here is to help the children with what they are really asking. Answer questions literally, not with background and nuance and extra information. They don't need the whole story that you hope they will ultimately have. That will take years!

- *Don't always expect to come up with the perfect response instantly.* Sometimes, even when you give what you think is the ideal answer, the child's response indicates that it wasn't. And that's okay. Even experts often need time to think about what a child really means and what response is likely to have a positive influence. There are no foolproof answers, because every child and situation is different. It's okay to say, "Hmm, I'm not sure what to say about that. Let me think about it and we can talk about it later."

- *When you respond to your child, take the age, prior experiences, specific needs, and unique concerns of your child into account.* As you saw in Chapter 3, children won't understand what they see and hear the way you do. The younger they are, the less logical and the more fragmented their thinking. You don't need to give them all the information at once—only what they seem to be asking for. And they won't necessarily understand everything you tell them, no matter how carefully you explain it.

- *A good way to respond to an issue your child raises is to try to find out what he knows.* Open-ended questions can help with this. For instance, if your child asks a question of a sexual nature, rather than jumping in with the "right" answer, try asking, "What have you heard about that?" How your child responds can guide what you say next. Such conversations can ensure that your little boy doesn't end up getting the whole birds-and-bees lecture when he asks you, "Where did I come from?" after his friend said he was from Minneapolis. And when your nine-year-old asks you, "What is oral sex? I think I know but I want to be sure," asking her what she thinks may lead to the response that one mother got: "It's when you talk about sex"! Examples of adults having more detailed give-and-take interactions with children are given in Chapter 6.

6. Encourage children to use play, art, and writing to process sexual images and other media messages they see.

Play, art, and writing activities provide children with endless possibilities for working on pressing problems and concerns and figuring out how to solve them. Not only do these activities help children work out ideas and feelings, they are also one of the most effective ways to protect children from developing problem-solving deficit disorder. Pay attention to and talk with children about their games and art. Listen to what they say to one another. Try to find out what they know and what confuses them. Providing open-ended (versus highly structured) play materials—such as blocks, baby dolls, generic dress-up clothes for male and female roles, miniature people, a doctor's kit and dollhouse, markers and paper—can support children's efforts to understand their relationships and their environment. James's kindergarten teacher provided opportunities for children to draw and write on a daily basis about what was on their minds. This created the avenue James needed to raise his concern about the "professional wrestling girl."

WHAT YOU CAN DO
To Help Children Use Play and
Art to Meet Their Needs

- *Provide toys and play materials that can be used in many ways rather than highly structured toys (toys that come with "scripts," like TV or* movie-themed action figures or characters) that control children's play. Highly structured toys can:

- Undermine play, creativity, and imagination as children use the toys to imitate the limited behavior suggested by the toy.
- Keep children's play focused on the theme suggested by the structure of the toy, thereby creating an unhealthy emphasis in their play on sexy appearance (as with Bratz dolls) or fighting (as with a *Star Wars* action figure).
- Channel children into narrowly defined behaviors for girls and for boys, thereby limiting the interests and skills they develop.
- Lead children to an exaggerated focus on consumerism—the desire to continually buy more and the belief that specific toys are needed in order to have fun and play "right."

- *Establish structures and routines that are conducive to encouraging creative play. For instance:*

  - Create regular, uninterrupted times during the day or week when your child has a chance to "just play." Some parents find that between dinner and bedtime is a good time for this. They often watch and even become involved with the activities themselves. This helps them learn more about what's on their children's minds and what they might want to try to influence.
  - Set up an uncluttered, well-organized place where your child's toys and play materials are readily available. This lets your child know that you value play. You can make picture labels on toy containers so your little girl can find what she wants to use and clean up after herself. Having crayons, markers, and paper in the kitchen lets your son draw and chat with you while you are making a meal.

- *Help your child get beyond narrowly scripted play that is controlled by a TV or movie script or highly structured play materials. For example, you can:*

- Introduce a more open-ended toy to be used with structured toys. For instance, using play dough with a Barbie doll might lead to fixing the doll a meal or making a birthday cake instead of just having fashion shows and going on dates.

- Get involved with the play without taking it over. Being a part of the fashion show and then saying you're hungry and need to have some lunch or are sleepy and need to go to bed can get your child focused on pretending to cook you a meal or making you a bed to sleep in. This introduces whole new elements into the play beyond the fashion show. After the play session, talk about the play with your child. Ask questions ("I wonder why Jasmine [a Bratz doll] always goes on dates? What else does she like to do?"). Compare what happened in the play to what might happen in your child's own life ("Barbie always worries about how she looks. Do you know anyone who spends so much time getting dressed?"). Comment on the stereotypes ("I notice that it's always the male characters who go out and fight. I wonder why that is?").

- Make sure you have time in your daily routine to play and have fun with your children. Too often, time to play with children is one of the first things that goes when schedules get too busy and too many demands seem to take over your life. But playing with your children is an important way to let them know that you value their play. It's a way to learn what they're interested in and share in it with them. As you play together, let the children keep control of the play; take the lead from them about what and how to play.

7. Counteract the narrow stereotypes of girls and boys that are so prevalent in media and commercial culture.

Children's potential to develop fully is greatly limited when they are channeled into a very narrow range of attitudes, behaviors, and skills according to gender. The more children define gender using the stereotyped images of popular culture—violence and macho behavior for boys, sexiness and helplessness for girls—the more limited their own view of themselves will be, as well as their view of the other gender. Whatever inherent differences might exist between males and females are so amplified by our popular culture, it's impossible to know what girls and boys would be like in a less gender-stereotyped world.

WHAT YOU CAN DO
To Reduce Gender Stereotypes

- *Focus on what your children do, not on how they look.* Avoid focusing on your children's appearance and clothing as long as you can. You may have to explain this to relatives and friends who are not as sensitized to the issue as you are.

- *Encourage a broad range of interests and skills in both your girls and your boys.* Ask your son to help you cook; get your daughter outside to play baseball. Have your kids help you pick and arrange flowers, as well as rake and bag leaves. Mix activities up; avoid stereotypes.

- *Choose toys and play materials that allow for a broad range of play activities instead of narrowly scripting them.* As mentioned above, play dough, blocks, dollhouses, doctors' kits, and crayons or markers and paper are wonderfully open-ended, allowing kids to create and role-play in ways that are not scripted and/or that will demonstrate to an observant parent what script a child *is* following. Teachers Resisting Unhealthy Children's Entertainment (TRUCE), an organization co-founded by Diane in the 1990s, prepares a Toy Action Guide for parents every year before the December holiday season. TRUCE is listed in the Resources section.

- *Encourage girls and boys to find common ground for engaging in meaningful activities with one another, including play.* Suggest they act out some aspect of a book you read to them, such as going on a boat trip to where the wild things are after reading Maurice Sendak's well-known book. Put on a puppet show using simple gender-neutral sock puppets onto which you can sew two buttons for eyes. Put a sheet over a table to create an enclosure—it can be a house, a cave, a tent, a store, a restaurant—whatever might be meaningful to the children based on their experience and interests. Add a few simple props based on the theme they decide, such as pots and pans for cooking at a restaurant or empty food containers if it's a store.

In these times, there are many forces that drive boys and girls into gender-divided play. There are plenty of gender-neutral things they can do together that can help them develop a broader range of interests and skills as well as a broader range of friends.

- *Consciously work against the narrow stereotypes that boys and girls see.* Help boys learn a broad range of alternatives to tough and violent behavior—including being caring and affectionate. Help girls work on alternatives to a focus on appearance and sexiness, such as being physically active and independent and engaging in play that goes beyond an emphasis on appearance.

- *Point out examples of males and females who are doing a broad range of activities, not just the limited range that children so often see in the media.* This includes serving as a role model yourself. When you're out in the community, you could comment positively on men pushing strollers or women police officers. When the TV is on, you might talk about women and men in roles that get beyond the stereotypes children usually see—female doctors, astronauts, and athletes, male nurses and flight attendants.

- *Help boys and girls find appealing role models that provide alternative images to increasingly influential celebrity culture with its superstar icons.* Talk about the leaders in your community—mayors, principals, civic leaders, and community helpers—so your child will become familiar with these roles and the people in them. Comment on acts of generosity, kindness, and compassion both in real life and in the media.

8. *Counteract compassion deficit disorder by helping children learn how to have positive and caring relationships.*

The more children experience the attitudes, values, and skills of having positive and caring relationships—i.e., those your culture values rather than those of the sexualized commercial culture—the better equipped they will be to resist negative messages that teach them to treat themselves and others as objects to be judged by how they look.

WHAT YOU CAN DO
To Teach Children How to
Have Positive Relationships

- *Give your children many direct opportunities to experience positive and caring relationships at home and at school.* To become adults capable of having caring relationships, including those that involve sex, children need to experience connected, give-and-take relationships throughout their childhood. They get these from the relationships they have with you and other important adults in their lives as well as from how they see the important adults in their lives relating to and supporting each other, including seeing them express warmth and affection.

- *Help children express and receive appropriate positive affection, both physical and otherwise, with important people in their lives.* Learning age-appropriate ways to express caring and affection for others—such as lending a helping hand, asking for and receiving help, and giving or receiving a hug or a pat on the back—can pave the way for later sexual experiences within the context of positive relationships.

- *Share stories about yourself and experiences you had at ages similar to your child's age.* These can be stories about a special friend, a favorite toy or play activity, or how you solved a problem with your parents, with a friend, or at school. Such accounts provide a powerful way to build your relationship with your child. They also can model how to think through issues and solve problems thoughtfully. Choose stories that relate to your children's experiences at their current age. Remember: Resist the impulse to lecture, and feel free to admit your mistakes!

9. *When conflicts arise between you and your children about sexuality and related issues, seek mutually agreeable solutions.*

There will be many times, especially as your children get older, when you won't agree on the same solution to an issue or problem. In these situations, it is too easy to threaten punishment in order to get your child to accept your point of view. Even if this succeeds in the short run, it won't help your child very much in the long run. The more you and your children are able to talk about disagreements, consider different points of view, and reach some sort of compromise, the more your children will learn how to think through issues and come up with responsible solutions when you are not there to do it with them.

WHAT YOU CAN DO
To Create a Give-and-Take Process for
Working Out Problems Together

- *Talk about the problem together in a way that helps your child see both sides.* For instance, you might say to your nine-year-old, "I can hear that you really want to go to that movie with your friends. A lot of them are going to see it, but it is rated PG-13 because of violence and sex. You know I don't feel it's okay for you to see movies like that without me there."

• *Look for one or more possible solutions that take into account both of your views.* In the above situation, you might say, "I guess now that all your friends are seeing the movie, we need to work out a new approach to PG-13 movies. I know you really want to go with your friends, but what if this time you and I go to see it together and then have a chance to talk about it?"

• *After your child has tried out the solution, talk together about how well it worked and decide what changes might be needed to make it work better next time.* For instance, after the movie, you and your daughter might have a discussion about the movie, what you both liked and didn't like about it, things that bothered either of you, and whether you both agree that seeing the movie was okay for someone your child's age, as well as what the solution might be next time such a situation comes up.

10. Share your values and concerns with other caring adults— your friends and relatives, and the parents of your children's friends.

In today's world, having a village really can help you raise your child! Being part of a supportive community can help you protect your children from exposure to the popular culture. It can be effective in developing a set of shared goals and values that are conveyed to all of its children. It can develop helpful responses as problems and concerns arise with your child. Few parents today have this kind of village. There almost seems to be an unspoken rule of silence among parents (and between schools and parents) when it comes to supporting each other's efforts to deal with media and popular culture, and *it has got to stop!* The silence serves the interests of marketers, not of you and your children.

Starting conversations with other adults about your experiences and concerns can build a community of adults who share the same values and support one another's efforts to promote healthy development in all the children. These conversations, big and small, can help you figure out where other adults stand on the issues and determine who your allies are and who might be unreliable. They can also confirm the validity of your concerns or help you see where you might be overreacting.

WHAT YOU CAN DO
To Work Cooperatively with Other Adults

- *Talk with other adults in your child's life about concerns and how you are trying to address them.* This means speaking with grandparents, aunts and uncles, childcare providers, babysitters, neighbors, teachers, and parents of your children's friends.

- *Don't always expect agreement.* Some parents and relatives will not share your values and concerns. They may be desensitized to the issues or perhaps simply resigned to the present situation. They may feel overwhelmed by other life demands.

- *Use the same give-and-take process for having conversations with other adults as we recommend with your children.* This approach optimizes the opportunity for everyone to have a voice, share information, and reach agreements when attitudes and ideas conflict.

- *Talk about specific issues that have come up with your child and how you have worked on resolving them.* This can be a less threatening way to raise issues with other adults, to help them see your point of view, and to model the problem-solving approach to working with children.

- *Agree on how you'll deal with TV and other media when your children are at one another's houses.* This one isn't always easy. Few parents have had much practice talking about these issues with one another. It's hard to stick up for what you care about without sounding judgmental about others' policies and putting them on the defensive. Just because your kids are friends doesn't mean you know their parents—or like them—all that much. Also, your attempts to get involved can seem increasingly as if you're trying to micromanage your children's lives as they get older.

A way to begin might be to casually verbalize your thinking and hopes for TV and video consumption on playdates without being pushy or rigid—"Hey, how do you deal with X, Y, or Z program? Has it been an issue for you? We've decided not allow it in our house because of . . . I hope that won't be a problem . . ."

- *Know where you want to draw the line.* Some disagreements won't seem worth making a big deal about and you may decide you can let your child live with them. Others will matter a lot to you; for these you may have to take a stand and limit your child's participation in a particular activity. Since consistency is key with kids of all ages, you should think now about what you will tolerate and what you can't allow. Your conviction in setting and sticking to limits, as long as they continue to work the way you want, will serve you well.

11. Ask your child's school to take seriously its vital role in working with children and families to help counteract the harm caused by the sexualization of childhood.

Schools that say it's all the parents' responsibility to protect their children from the negative influences of the media and popular culture need assistance to change. Too often, schools are sacrificing opportunities to help children develop social knowledge and skills in favor of intensified academic instruction. An important first step is getting schools to acknowledge that when children reveal in school that they have seen or been influenced by something that schools deem inappropriate, it's not solely the parents' fault. Schools can create an atmosphere in which parents and teachers, as well as parents and parents, can talk and learn from one another about how to limit children's exposure to potentially harmful media and cultural influences and deal with the effects. When this happens, it's a win-win situation for everyone but the marketers. In addition, it's a win for education. When children's thoughts, feelings, and energy are consumed by trying to negotiate the minefields of the sexualized popular culture, they're not nearly as able to learn what schools are trying to teach. Schools must get involved. The more parents and teachers can support each other on this issue, the better off children will be.

WHAT YOU CAN DO
To Help Parents and Schools Work Together

- *Build parent-teacher relationships based on mutual respect and collaboration.* Finding an approach that fits the diversity of children and their families is not always easy. Parents and teachers will have a wide range of perspectives on sexualization issues. As you begin to work together, it's important to provide opportunities for different points of view to be voiced and to try to find common ground for working together. The more you succeed at creating an ongoing process for dealing with concerns together, the easier the job is for everyone. The same give-and-take approach for having discussions with schools described in the previous section can also be used effectively in having discussions with other parents.

- *Parents and teachers can share concerns with one another about issues that arise in school related to the sexualization of childhood.* Teachers can use situations such as how girls are dressing, comments about the media they are seeing, or boyfriend/girlfriend issues as opportunities to work with and educate parents. Parents can share situations that come up at home, such as makeover birthday parties for girls or remarks by boys or girls about the sexy girl in the class. If the situation involves only an individual child, sometimes a conference or phone call or letter can do the trick. When several children are involved, the solution might be a newsletter home or an evening for parents. Together parents and teachers can try to develop concrete solutions and share the burden.

• *Work to create a schoolwide community that makes dealing with the sexualization of childhood a communitywide affair.* Plan parent meetings with guest speakers who can help the whole community better understand sexualization, commercialization, and media is- sues in their children's lives, and what to do about them. Set up meetings so parents can talk with their children's teachers and support one another's efforts. One parent was very grateful when her child's teacher got parents talking about appropriate birthday gifts. Parents and their children became much more careful when choosing gifts for other children. This also led some parents to talk to relatives about the issue. Schools should work to provide par- ents with information and resources that will help them do their job at home. The Resources section at the end of the book will help you do this.

• *You can ask your children's teachers and school administrators to keep parents informed about issues that come up in school related to the sexualized culture and what is being done about them.* Suggest they use these incidents as teaching opportunities rather than sources of guilt, shame, or punishment or pretending they didn't occur. For instance, we heard of a classroom that had a problem when the girls brought in Bratz dolls and the boys decapitated them on the playground! The teacher led a give-and-take conversation with the children about the seriousness of the problem and their reac- tions. The children and the teacher discussed what girls like about

Bratz dolls, differences between what boys and girls like, what is and isn't okay to do when you disagree about what you like, and what to do to make things better. This teacher also wrote a letter home to parents about the incident and the discussion that followed. A more punitive teacher might have taken away the boys' recess for a week or sent them to the principal's office, whereby little would have been learned by either side.

• *Get parents and teachers (and, as appropriate and relevant, children too) to work outside the home and school to reduce the nature and amount of sexualized content in media and popular culture.* Use individual and group letters, petitions, phone calls, and other actions to local retailers, TV stations, advertisers, and toy and clothing manufacturers to voice specific concerns. Many of the specific action steps outlined in the Conclusion will help with this.

A QUICK REVIEW OF WHAT YOU CAN DO

1. Protect children as much as possible from exposure to sexual imagery and related content in the media and popular culture.

2. Learn about the media and popular culture in your child's life—popular TV programs, movies, video and computer games, fashion, celebrities.

3. Get beyond the "Just say no" approach.

4. Establish safe channels for talking about sexual development and related issues with children, starting when they are very young.

5. Make age-appropriate give-and-take conversations about sexualization of childhood issues an essential part of your relationship with your child.

6. Encourage children to use play, art, and writing to process sexual images and other media messages they see.

7. Counteract the narrow stereotypes of boys and girls that are so prevalent in media and commercial culture.

8. Counteract compassion deficit disorder by helping children learn how to have positive and caring relationships.

9. When conflicts arise between you and your child about sexuality and related issues, seek mutually agreeable solutions.

10. Share your values and concerns with other caring adults— your friends and relatives, and the parents of your children's friends.

11. Ask your child's school to take seriously its vital role in working with children and families to help counteract the harm caused by the sexualization of childhood.

Chapter 6

Working It Out Together

The Power of Connecting Deeply with Children

BEING THERE THROUGH THICK AND THIN

To bring the guidelines in Chapter 5 to life, let's return to Hannah, last seen crying in the bathtub in Chapter 1, and see what Jennifer, her mother, does. No adult, even an expert in child development, would find it easy to figure out an effective response to Hannah's distress. Fortunately, Jennifer has created a relationship with her that makes Hannah feel safe in telling her mother what is upsetting her.

As unsure as she is about the right way to respond, Jennifer knows she has to plunge in anyway. Their give-and-take conversation (which follows) captures very powerfully how a parent can create a sense of safety for children and help them deal with many complex issues. Here it is, along with commentary about what we think Jennifer is teaching and Hannah is learning.

Hannah and Jennifer's Give-and-Take Conversation

Conversation	Commentary
Hannah (crying in the bathtub): I'm fat! I'm fat! I want to be pretty like Isabelle . . . sexy like her!	• Hannah feels it is safe to say exactly what she is feeling about her body.
Jennifer: It sounds like you're really upset about your body, about how it looks.	• Jennifer focuses on what Hannah says and feels and acknowledges it without injecting her own ideas yet.
Hannah: Yes. I'm fat. I told you I'm fat before. I told you I want to go on a diet. I *need* a diet.	• Jennifer's "active listening" helps Hannah feel safe saying more about what she really thinks and feels.
Jennifer: So you think that a diet will help you change how you look?	• Jennifer focuses on trying to figure out the meaning that "going on a diet" has for Hannah.
Hannah: Yes! It will! Jemma says she's on a diet with her mother.	• Hannah seems relieved that Jennifer "gets it" and provides more useful information.
	• Jennifer makes a note to herself to try to find a tactful way to talk to Jemma's mother, Ruth, about the diet and why they decided to diet together. Could Ruth be having similar issues with Jemma as she's been having with Hannah?

Jennifer: So you and your friends are talking about going on diets? What do you know about diets?

- Without making value judgments or voicing her own opinions, she asks an open-ended question to try to find out more about what Hannah knows.

Hannah: A diet is when you only eat a little . . . a little bit at every meal. I eat too much! You shouldn't let me.

- Hannah reveals that her concept of diet focuses on *how much* you eat, not *what* you eat. At age seven, this is the easier concept to understand.

Jennifer: So you think I should help you be on a diet . . . to eat less food at every meal?

- Young children see their parents as the center of the universe—as the ones who can control what happens.

Hannah: Yes!!! I want to be pretty.

- In her mind, Hannah has linked eating less with being prettier and probably skinnier. She is focusing on the before-and-after "slides" or frames of the movie, but doesn't seem to be thinking about how to get from Slide A to Slide B.

Jennifer: Sweetie, it sounds like you think you're not pretty, and if you eat less, you'll be prettier. How does that work?

- Jennifer holds back on her desire to contradict Hannah's view about her prettiness, and instead stays focused on how Hannah thinks.
- Helping Hannah put her thinking about diets and bodies into words, and making connections between her various ideas, can

Hannah: You know . . . you get skinny when you eat less. That's prettier, sexier.

- Jennifer learns more about what diets mean to Hannah; she discovers that Hannah focuses on quantity, not on the kinds of food eaten. And Hannah makes a one-to-one *relationship* between being skinny, pretty, and sexy.

Jennifer: So you want to get skinnier because that will make you sexy? What do you know about "sexy"?

- Jennifer reflects back what Hannah said in order to show Hannah she understands what was said. She also seeks more information about what "sexy" means, thereby avoiding making it an emotionally loaded issue.

Hannah: Sexy is when you're pretty so boys like you. You run around and they try to catch you. They even kiss you 'cause they like you. That's what happens with Isabelle.

- Hannah shows she's on the right track in her understanding of "sexy"—but still has a seven-year-old way of thinking about it. She realizes looking sexy connects with physical behavior, such as kissing.

Jennifer: Wow! I'm glad you're talking to me about this. You know, I've always liked the way you look. But I want to help *you* feel okay about your looks.

- Jennifer lets Hannah know that it is okay to talk with her about these things. She also uses this talk as an opportunity to inject what she thinks about the subject and guide Hannah's thinking. She does it in a way that doesn't put Hannah down for her feelings and thoughts. And she makes sure Hannah realizes

help her reach a more advanced level of thinking.

that she's there to help Hannah solve this (and other) problems.

Hannah: I told you—that's why I want to go on a diet. Eat less.

- As many seven-year-olds might, Hannah focuses on only one aspect of the situation—dieting.

Jennifer: Yes, and you said you want me to help you. How could that work?

- Taking the lead, Jennifer focuses on diet as the place to begin helping Hannah work on her "problem." This does not mean they won't talk about other possible solutions later.

Hannah: You give me less food to eat.

- Hannah assumes her mother is the provider of her food; Jennifer gets the job of making the diet happen.

Jennifer: So here's an idea. I'll talk to you . . . tell you which foods are the healthiest so you can eat the most of them.

- Hannah's thinking about diets is again like a slide—"Here's the one thing I do to be on a diet." Jennifer tries to turn the slide into a movie—"Here's how I can help you make decisions about what you eat and how much."

Hannah: Yeah. Then I'll get skinny.

- Jennifer tries to get the focus to be on healthy eating, but Hannah holds on to her focus of dieting to be skinny.

Jennifer: And if you want, when you go to the doctor for your

- Not giving up, but also not putting down what Hannah says, Jennifer

checkup next week, you can talk to her about whether she thinks you should be thinner. She has a special chart that shows her how many pounds children your age and your height should weigh to be healthy.

tries to *complicate her thinking.* By bringing the family pediatrician into the discussion, she connects the issue of being skinny with health and lets Hannah know her doctor can play a role in helping Hannah solve the problem.

Jennifer and Hannah's conversation illustrates how the process for working out problems together outlined in Chapter 5 can work in practice. Jennifer feels pleased and relieved that the conversation accomplished her goals. Hannah knows her mother has heard her unhappiness and can help her do something about it. The conversation opened up a whole line of discussion that had never occurred before, about bodies, appearance, and sexuality, that Jennifer knows will serve them both well as future issues inevitably arise.

This kind of connection is vital for children to have with their parents as children encounter the hazards of today's world. Jennifer has learned more about how issues of diet, body image, friendships, sex, and sexuality all interact with one another in Hannah's seven-year-old mind. Most important of all, Hannah now knows that it's okay to talk to her mother about her problems and that her mother will help her try to find solutions.

Of course, this conversation in the bathroom is just the beginning. Pandora's box has been opened. There are likely to be many more conversations to come about issues related to Hannah's body and sexuality. And Jennifer will never be able to predict exactly where they will lead. But, as difficult as these conversations may be, children need to know that the important adults in their lives are allies who are there to assist them in their efforts to deal with a sexually charged culture. And it is clear that Jennifer understands this.

THE BIRDS AND THE BEES GET MORE
AND MORE COMPLICATED

You will have noticed that the issues that Jennifer and Hannah talked about are more closely related to sexiness than to sex. In the midst of all the complex sexual information children need to process these days, they also still need to learn positive information about the birds and the bees. The following story shows how, over several years, a father and son talked about issues more directly connected to sex. This story also illustrates how the basic sex education information children get interacts in a child's mind with more highly charged and less appropriate sexual messages from the popular culture.

Seth and His Dad Work It Out Together

Conversation	Commentary
• When Seth is five years old, seemingly out of the blue he asks Dave, his father, "How do babies get into the mother?" Trying to provide just the information Seth is asking for, Dave succinctly says, "The father puts a seed in the mother and the baby starts to grow." "Oh," replies Seth, and then he walks away.	• Young children commonly ask questions about the origins of babies. But, as we see with Seth, they come up with their own ways of asking their questions based on their unique experiences and level of development.
	• Dave's response gives Seth just the information he is asking for. He stops to see if Seth wants more. Seth seems to be satisfied with the one-slide answer and is not looking for a movie or entire slide show.
	• By his response, Dave is showing it's safe to ask grown-ups such questions.

- About a year and a half later, seemingly picking up on the previous conversation where it left off, Seth returns to his father and asks, "But how does the father put the seed in the mother so the baby starts to grow?" With similar directness Dave replies, "The dad puts his penis between the mother's legs into her vagina and the seed goes in." Again Seth walks away and continues what he had been doing before asking the question. Dave wonders if what he has said is helpful, confusing, or disturbing to Seth, or all of the above. Should he try to keep the conversation going?

- With advances in age and thinking, Seth is now trying to *make a movie* about how babies are made.
- Once again, Dave gives only the information Seth is asking for. He is honest about what happens and uses anatomically correct terminology.
- Since Seth seems comfortable asking questions when he needs to, Dave is probably right in waiting to see what Seth does next.

- It's not until about six months later that Seth again approaches Dave. This time, instead of a question, Seth blurts out, "I really want to be a dad and have a baby when I grow up. But I'm not going to do that thing with my penis and the mother." At first speechless, Dave quickly regroups and replies, "I know that's hard for children to understand. But when two grown-ups really love each other, they like to do it and it feels special and good." Seth asks, "Is that sex?" Dave replies, "Yes. That's what sex is."

- Seth's level of thinking is definitely advancing. He is making a movie in his head now. He's more able to use logical reasoning about cause and effect. He is also now thinking about what the movie he has made means for himself. But at age seven, there are still limitations to his thinking that make his conclusions quite understandable. He focuses on the concrete—the sex act itself. He can't imagine what he can't see—feelings that underlie a caring relationship in which sex is a part.

- About a year later, when Seth is almost eight, things get more complicated. He comes home from school one afternoon and asks his father, "Is 'sexy' sex?" Unsure what Seth is really asking, this time Dave responds with a question, "Did you hear about sexy at school?" "Yes," Seth replies. To get more information, Dave follows up with an open-ended question that can have many answers: "What did you hear about it?" Seth says, "Joel said Monica's 'sexy' and he likes her." Aha! Now Dave has a better sense of what Seth is getting at. So he explains, "There are lots of reasons why people become friends and like each other. Sometimes you might find the way someone looks—attractive, pretty, sexy—gets you interested in finding out more. But sexy is different from sex, because sex isn't for children."

- Finally, when Seth is eight and a half, something happens that upsets Dave and clearly is also up-

- Dave acknowledges Seth's feelings. He tries to give Seth simple, honest information that he hopes will reassure him.

- As the peer group becomes a more powerful force in children's lives, it gets harder for parents to protect children from the popular culture. That's why it's important to have already established deep and trusting connections for talking about important issues when children are young.

- Dave is using open-ended questions to try to find out more about what Seth's question means. It also buys him time to figure out how to answer! It would also have been okay for Dave to buy more time by saying, "Let me think about that and talk to you more about it tomorrow."

- Dave realizes that the birds and the bees and the pop culture have begun to connect for Seth. Wisely, he focuses on the *objectification* issue to convey his values about relationships, but he doesn't ignore the "sexy" part either.

- As children get older, children of even the most conscientious parents have access to more and

setting to Seth. Here's Dave's account of what happened: "I was sitting with Seth after lights-out. He said he had something to tell me and he hoped I wouldn't be mad. He had seen something on the Internet that he shouldn't have seen and it worried him. His friend Alex had shown him some 'sexy stuff' on the computer. I responded by asking Seth what he saw. He said, 'Bare breasts and a man putting his penis in a woman's mouth.' Seth added that at some points he looked away because he didn't like looking at what was on the screen. At first, I was at a loss about what to do. I settled on trying to focus on the context—explaining to him that some grown-ups like to look at pictures of bodies with no clothes and sex, but it's *not* something his mom or I like to do, and it's not something for children to see and I don't think grown-ups should have things like that on the Internet that children can find."

• Next, Dave focused on the specific situation with Seth and Alex in the here and now: "I asked

more of the sexualized media and commercial culture.

• This situation graphically illustrates how all that happened earlier between Seth and Dave succeeded in paving the way for Seth to know he can go to Dave for help when something comes up related to sex that upsets him.

• Dave uses an open-ended question to find out more and to give himself a minute to think about what to say.

• More and more children are viewing Internet pornography at younger and younger ages. Dave and Seth's discussion is one of the few instances we have heard of in which a parent and child discuss it so openly. It's something all parents need to learn how to do.

• With increasing age, as Seth's experience and level of thinking grow, with each discussion we can see Dave talking more and more directly about the sexual aspects of Seth's questions.

• Dave tries to bring in his values as well as to create boundaries between adults and children.

• Dave tries to use the discussion as a teaching opportunity, helping Seth build skills for resisting peer

Seth what he could have done when Alex offered to show him the Internet pictures with sex. Could he have told Alex he didn't want to see them? I explained that this is why we have the special program on our computer at home so that children can't see the things that are for grown-ups. I ended by saying, 'It can be really hard to know what decision to make for yourself when your mom or I aren't there to help with it.' "

pressure that will be increasingly helpful in the future.

- A couple of days later, as Dave and his wife are still talking about how to talk to Alex's parents (not *whether* to talk to them), Seth comes home from school and reports that Alex's parents found out about the sex stuff and punished him. He lost all his "screen time" for a month!

- The contrast between Dave's response and Alex's parents' response dramatically captures the two extremes in how adults commonly deal with the sexualization of childhood with their children. By focusing only on setting limits and giving punishments, Alex's parents miss a crucial opportunity to help Alex deal with the pornography he saw and to influence the lessons he is learning. Their response also teaches Alex that it's not safe to talk to his parents about sexual issues.

The first part of Dave's account—answering Seth's questions about reproduction and sex—could have taken place ten or twenty years ago. There is nothing about it that stands out as being obviously influenced by the current sexualized environment. It illustrates appropriate and sensitive give-and-take interactions between a caring adult and a child who, bit by bit, is trying to figure out how the world works. Seth feels safe asking his father questions and telling him what he knows in a matter-of-fact, direct way. While Seth seems concerned about what he hears about intercourse between a man and a woman, he is able to talk to his father about his concerns, and Dave is doing just what the sexualized culture does not do—namely, connecting the act of sex and making babies to caring relationships between adults.

The latter part of Dave's account shows how the sexualized world of mainstream culture creeps into a child's life and how a child uses what he already knows to try to make sense of what he hears and sees. But perhaps most important of all, it shows how the trusting relationship between Dave and Seth—which made talking about sex and sexual issues safe and comfortable right from the start—allowed Seth to go to his father when sexual issues came up that puzzled or upset him. That trusting connection is the most important way you, as the adult who cares for children, can support their efforts to cope with the toxic environment and lay the foundation for them to grow up to be capable of having caring, intimate relationships that include sex.

BUILDING THE POWER TO RESIST: IT'S NOT EASY, BUT IT'S WORTH IT

Both Jennifer and Dave would have preferred not to have to deal with the sexualized real world entering their children's lives in such stressful ways. As a parent, you try to protect your children as much as you can from information and experiences that can upset them or teach them harmful lessons, or that they are not ready to understand. And it is appropriate to do so. But as Jennifer and Dave have shown, the sexualized messages from the outside world will get in, and when they do, there is much you can do to help your children. Once you begin, you may find that having these conversations, although difficult at times, becomes one of the most satisfying and meaningful aspects of your relationship with your child.

Beyond "No Child Left Behind"

Carrie, the teacher you read about in Chapter 4 who had a student who learned from the Disney Channel how to identify the popular children by the clothing they wore, also told us about how she has begun to understand and deal with the worrisome increase in the sexualized behavior she is seeing in her classroom. Although there's no magic formula for making things better, Carrie found that many little adaptations in how she conducts her classroom made a big difference, although not as big as she would like. She continues to learn as she goes. The excerpt below from her teaching journal captures what can be done when teachers have the understanding and commitment to work with parents and children to promote positive development of the whole child. It shows why there's so much more to teach children than just the three R's. As you'll see, even very experienced and thoughtful teachers find that the solutions don't just magically appear. Carrie shows a willingness to identify the areas where she herself needs to learn more. She is also willing to experiment and problem-solve, take risks, make mistakes, and change.

In the course of her efforts, you'll see a transformation in Carrie's understanding, as well as in her ability to respond to the needs of her students:

> Throughout that difficult year, I tried many strategies to counteract the negative impact that all these complicated social factors were having on our ability to live, learn, and laugh in the classroom. We had class meetings and made rules. Looking back, it started out with mostly me

making the rules with little student input, hoping that rules would make the sexualized and aggressive behaviors go away. Over time, I found that giving the children a voice in setting the rules (even when the rule we came up with wasn't exactly what I had in mind) worked a lot better. It gave the children a chance to form new ideas and arguments and buy into the new rules.

Since there was a very strong in-crowd that actively excluded other children, I tried partnering in-crowd children with classmates they didn't usually work with to try to help form new friendships and promote tolerance. I had lunch meetings with the powerful core group of apparent ringleaders to try to alter their exclusion of some children. I set up a series of meetings for my most involved kindergarten girls to meet with our counselor. I also worked a great deal with the children's parents and grandparents about what was going on, how we were dealing with it, and what they could do at home to help. I brainstormed with families and colleagues about new things we could try with the children and dedicated some of my weekly family newsletters to the topic.

One thing that worked really well was bringing back some of my former students, who had strong social skills when they were with me, to help create a positive counterculture. They led activities and participated in meetings where they modeled more inclusive behavior.

And I cried and yelled. Some strategies helped, but it was an ongoing, upward battle. Most days I would go home exhausted and often discouraged and worried as well.

On the upside, even with No Child Left Behind, which puts a lot of pressure on our school to follow a lockstep, Three-R-focused curriculum, the principal has managed to help teachers keep some degree of autonomy over what happens in their classrooms. Our five-, six-, and seven-year-old children still have time to play. They play with blocks and play dough, which doesn't happen in a lot of public school kindergartens and first grades anymore. They love to dress up, play with puppets, cuddle the baby dolls, and draw hearts. It's so wonderful when they succeed at letting go of all the grown-up baggage they bring and really just behave

129

like children. And even though I wish they didn't have the need, their play gives the children opportunities to exhibit the issues sexualization raises for them. Even the "coolest" kids will sing "The Pizza Song" and "Make New Friends." "Can we do it in a round?" they'll ask. It's very comforting to see that they still do know how to be "kids" doing what kids should be doing. I now have a new goal—helping the children be children, taking off the burden of needing to be too grown up too soon.

As the winter turned into spring, it suddenly hit me that media influences were at the heart of what I was seeing in the children. Once I realized this, I could see it everywhere. And by the end of the school year, it was crystal clear that the students were as confused as I was. They were confused about all the images they were seeing, and were trying to play them out and make sense of the world created by media with all the sex, sexiness, and violence they see. I decided to use the summer to try to learn more about media's influence on children and how to work with children and families on media literacy next year.

I will have many of these students again next year, so I'll have another year to build on what I started last year. This time, last year's kindergartners will be my returning role models. As first-graders they will help set the tone. Together we will get to know the incoming kindergartners. I have strong relationships with my returning students' families, and that will make it easier to continue the conversations we've begun. I'll have thought so much more about the media influences, and won't just be focusing on the behavior I am seeing. Today I am hopeful. Tomorrow, I don't know.

At the start of the following school year, Carrie was beginning to believe progress was possible:

We've had two days of school so far. I'm feeling very hopeful because they've gone so well. Not perfect, but successful, which is in stark contrast to how I ended last year. The media course I took over the summer has transformed the way I am dealing with the issues. I have more tools now for helping students and parents. I feel powerful now, in a way I didn't last year. By powerful, I mean equipped.

Here's an example from the second day of school that captures the transformation I feel. Robbie brought in a book based on the live-action and animated *Space Jam* movie. The PG-rated movie pits Bugs Bunny and his Looney Tunes friends against the alien Nerdlucks in a basketball game. Michael Jordan and other NBA stars appear in the movie to assist one side or the other. The book has cartoon images and still photos from the movie. There's lots of very small print on every page . . . way too hard for anyone in the class to actually read. Robbie brought the book out during "Quiet Reading" because he knew it would create a stir with other kids—and it did. Immediately, a small group of boys gathered around him on the rug. He tried hard to manage all their requests . . . to see the book, touch the pages, and choose what character they would be when they acted the movie out at playtime. I was sitting close by, trying to listen to a first-grader who wanted to read to me. She was getting frustrated because the boys were distracting me. Two kindergarten boys wanted to see the book and asked for my help. Then a first-grade boy began crying because he wanted to be a certain character that was already chosen. I kept asking the group to be quiet. They kept trying to hush themselves, but were too charged up about the book. Robbie was getting frustrated because he just wanted to use the book to tell the story, not worry about acting it out.

A part of me was happy he was pretending to read, real progress for him. I wanted to give Robbie the space to try to resolve the problem on his own. Then the girl reading to me started to cry. Now two kids were crying. The rest of the room was quiet and focused. I turned to Robbie and said, without raising my voice, "You know, Robbie, that book is getting seven or eight people really frustrated. Look, Laska's crying, Mehoe is crying." "I'm sad," said Robbie, and he hung his head low. "I'm going to take the book home." He stood up and crossed his arms tightly around the book. "I think that's a good idea, Robbie," I said. "You can look for another book in the room you'd like to read." And that's just what he did.

Those seven to ten minutes were critical for the children and for me. I know that last year I would've been quicker to tell Robbie to put the book away—to take it home and leave it there. He would've been upset with me. It wouldn't have really solved the issue. And he wouldn't have learned anything. This way, he found a way to gain control of the situation. Later in the day, when he was calmer and I had a few minutes, I sat down with Robbie and we talked about what happened and what he learned from it. He did most of the talking, with a few questions from me. It is a small victory for both of us, and stems directly from the tools I am trying from the media literacy class I took this summer.

What's clear to us here is that Carrie has stopped looking for "quick fix" rules that will solve the problems created by today's world, which is how too many adults try to deal with these problems. Instead, she uses her new understanding, gained from her experience with her students and the media literacy course, to build deeper connections with children, connections that will help them develop the resources and skills they need in order to resist at least some of the impact of sexualized and violent media culture. It is a journey that will continue for as long as she works with children.

A CRASH COURSE FOR CHILDREN (AND FAMILIES)

Now let's turn to older elementary-age children. Connie, whose concerns about pornography appearing in the lives of fifth- and sixth-graders you read about in Chapter 1, is the health education teacher at her school. The flyer sent home to families describes the health education program as

a curriculum designed to explore health, safety, and human development with students in grades prekindergarten through eight. Children are given concrete information about a wide range of subjects from human biology and psychology to keeping themselves safe. We provide a context in which children's questions, curiosities, or anxieties about any of life's complex issues can be explored in a supportive, straightforward manner, respectful of differences. . . . It is our goal for children to be empowered to make life-enhancing decisions that will impact their physical, emotional, and mental well-being. Self-esteem and respect for others are the top priorities.

The following excerpts are from newsletters Connie wrote to parents reporting on fifth- and sixth-grade growth education classes. These are the grades in which she focuses on body changes and puberty. She creates an environment where a broad range of issues can come up and where children feel safe asking their questions and sharing what they know. The classes alternate between single-gender and mixed groups. She keeps parents well informed about the issues that the children bring to the class and makes recommendations about how parents might respond if children raise these issues at home.

JANUARY 23 NEWSLETTER TO
5TH/6TH GRADE PARENTS

Dear 5/6 Parents,

We're about halfway through this year's growth ed program so I want to give you a sense of what we've covered and the flavor of the conversations. As in other areas of the curriculum some kids talk a lot and ask a lot of questions, others are more reserved. Some kids know a lot and others are just learning. I try to create a comfortable atmosphere and give everyone a chance to speak. Kids have the opportunity to put questions in the question box at the end of each session. I encourage you to talk to your kids about the issues described in this newsletter. If you have feedback for me, I would like to hear from you.

We have talked about body changes to expect during puberty. We talk about body image and media and cultural influences on body image. . . . One question that *always* comes up is: What are the mechanics of intercourse and specifically what would happen if the man peed inside the woman (it is a relief for them to hear that nature has designed things better than that).

All groups have talked about crushes. One thing that surprised me was that many of the girls seemed to feel that boys had to ask girls out or let girls know they liked them. When I questioned that idea, they referred to the media, especially the Harry Potter movie. This turned into a lively discussion about the advantages and disadvantages of being the asker and the asked. We talked about what it means in fifth/sixth grade to be asked out. Some kids said it meant going to the movies with just one person. Others said it was just something to gossip about and create a stir about. There was wondering about how you know when someone likes you. Kids gave different and, in some ways, conflicting answers: if someone's nice to you, if someone's really mean to you, if they sit near you or bump into you in the hall.

FEBRUARY 10 NEWSLETTER TO
5TH/6TH GRADE PARENTS

This week marked the end of our scheduled growth education classes. I always tell the kids that the end of classes shouldn't mean the end of questions. They know where the books are and know people they can go to for information and advice. One of the things I like best about teaching this subject is the feeling in the room when one kid risks saying something like, "What do you do if you have a crush on someone and you just know they're never going to like you back because they're older or so much better than you are?" Another kid chimes in, "Don't say that about yourself. Don't think other people are better than you are." And then another says, "I feel that way sometimes—like, right now!" There is a palpable sense of connectedness, of not being alone with tender feelings.

Since I last wrote, we've had conversations about physical attractiveness. Kids had a range of opinions from "It's how the person looks to *you* that's important" to "It's not true that it's personality that counts—it's how you look." This led to a discussion about ads. Someone said, "In ads, the sexy people are what people think is attractive. They aren't even real sometimes." This comment led to a discussion about media influence on body image and gender stereotypes. As we talked about stereotypes, I was struck when all the children agreed that at times boys are "afraid of strong feelings they don't know how to express so it comes out weird like teasing or joking."

Kids had questions about pornography—especially why someone would want to be in a picture or a movie like that. I talked about how for most people being sexual is a private thing. Children volunteered that people might do pornography if they needed money because they get paid to do it. Some kids had seen things they wondered or were worried about. I encouraged them to tell you when they see something confusing or upsetting. Now is a good time to ask your kids about what we're doing in growth ed and talk with them about some of these topics. It's so important they know that they can talk to you.

Connie's newsletters show how schools and caring teachers can work with children in thoughtful, responsible, and deeply connected ways to promote positive lessons about sex and sexuality and counteract the harm caused by the sexualized environment. The way Connie works with children models how educators can lay the foundation for caring relationships and healthy sex and sexuality.

CHILDREN'S RIGHT, SCHOOLS' RESPONSIBILITY

Carrie's and Connie's efforts show how teachers' work with children on issues discussed in this book can be incorporated into schools and can progress in content and sophistication with the age of the child. Carrie's and Connie's teaching provides a standard to which all schools should be expected to aspire. They stand out in sharp contrast to the abstinence-only approach to sex education that is promoted today in too many schools in the United States. Children, families, and society would all be in a far better place, in spite of today's toxic cultural environment, if there were more educators like Carrie and Connie working with children and families.

The more families and schools succeed at providing children with the kinds of experiences they need to process and counteract the lessons today's sexualized childhood teaches them, the better prepared they will be to resist the pressures that they will soon confront when they enter adolescence. But in this sexualized environment there is still much to deal with as children get older. Although this book is primarily about early childhood, we also want to discuss what happens to sexualized children as they enter adolescence and how we can help them, and this is where we now turn.

Chapter 7

The Sexualized Child
Enters Adolescence

The Floodgates Open

If your children are young and you take the advice in Chapters 5 and 6, you'll be in a very good position to stay connected with them as they become adolescents. You will have become an askable parent and will have laid the foundation for conversations on every imaginable topic—and some you can't possibly imagine. If your children are already teenagers, don't despair! It is never too late to begin the conversation. You can't control your teenager, but you can still establish connections that will help him or her develop good instincts and sound values and resist the destructive messages of the sexualized commercial culture.

It has become normal in our culture for teenagers to rebel, for adolescence to be a time of conflict between children and parents, and for the older generation to be shocked, troubled, and mystified by the ways of the younger generation. If you weren't faced with a premature adolescent rebellion earlier, it's likely that rebellion issues will come up now. But just as childhood is dramatically different today than it used to be, so is the world of adolescence.

Nowhere is this difference more striking than in the media environment. Rapid advances in technology have made readily available to most American children devices and methods of communication that, if imagined at all, belonged to the world of science fiction not that long ago—the Internet, cell phones, handheld computers, e-mail, text messaging, hundreds of cable channels, CDs, DVDs, iPods, and more. This new technology, along with the predominance of the marketplace and a more tolerant culture, has snapped up the shades on hundreds of windows that used to be off-limits to most children and teenagers. You saw in Chapter 2 many of the harmful messages that young children get from the media. As you'll see, these messages escalate dramatically as children grow older.

MESSAGES ABOUT SEX AND GENDER IN THE POPULAR CULTURE

One fine spring afternoon, fifteen-year-old Matt burst onto the street with a sawed-off shotgun, just as the friendly neighborhood cop was riding by on his bicycle. Matt shot the cop, commandeered the bike, broke out his Glock, and streaked down the street firing indiscriminately at passersby. In the chaos, a car exploded, flinging a flaming construction worker across the street. Matt decided to ditch the bike. Blowing away the driver of a car with his shotgun, he dragged him onto the sidewalk and peeled off in the car. He spotted a young woman in a very short skirt on the side of the road and ordered her to get in. He drove her to a remote spot and had intercourse with her in the backseat of the car. When he was finished with her, he dragged her out of the car and stomped her to death, feeling himself get hard again as he watched her die. Then his mother ruined everything by calling up the stairs and asking him to set the table.

Matt was playing *Grand Theft Auto,* one of the most popular video games of all time—a game so socially acceptable and widely known that Coca-Cola did a commercial based on an imitation of it. Millions of teenage boys while away hours every day playing this game and others of its ilk. And then they go to school, where they encounter lots of girls wearing very short skirts.

While Matt was on his murderous spree, his thirteen-year-old sister, Lizzie, was lying on her bed reading *Cosmopolitan*. She was learning about how to give a great blow job. Her best friend, Rachel, had gone to a party on Saturday night and told Lizzie all about it. The most popular girl in the class had gone down on three of the football players. Lizzie thought it sounded gross, but Rachel said it was cool. Lizzie didn't think she'd know how to do it and she didn't want to ask Rachel, but she'd found the answer in *Cosmo*. It did sound gross, though.

How we wish we were making all this up, but we aren't. These are some of the messages that tweens and teens are getting from the popular culture. Boys who played with *Mighty Morphin Power Rangers* and *Masters of the Universe* "graduate" to *Grand Theft Auto*. Little Sasha who loved the Bratz dolls (in Chapter 2) may increasingly want to *become* one. Gabe, who stumbled upon traditional pornography (in Chapter 1), will probably need something more exciting, more aberrant, as he becomes a teenager. Desensitization means they have to keep upping the ante.

Why is this happening? As we've said, a commercial culture that sexualizes and objectifies children and that glorifies casual sex in order to increase profits is a major factor. Although the federal government spends more than $175 million annually to promote abstinence education in schools, popular culture is still the leading source of sex education in the nation. And it creates a climate that encourages a very cavalier attitude toward sex. We could write a whole other book about the impact of the media on teenagers, but this chapter will have to be a crash course. Here are just a few of these media messages:

Advertising

Young people are extremely desirable to advertisers because they are new consumers, are beginning to have significant disposable income, and are developing brand loyalty that might last a lifetime. Teenagers spend $155 billion a year on a wide variety of products. Teenage girls spend over $8 billion annually on beauty products alone.

As we all know, sex has long been used in advertising to sell just about everything—from champagne to shampoo, chain saws to chewing gum. These days, however, graphic sexual images are more extreme, more pervasive, and more perverse than ever before. In 1980 Calvin Klein caused quite a stir with a commercial featuring the then fifteen-year-old Brooke Shields purring, "Nothing comes between me and my Calvins." That ad would seem tame today.

Images that used to belong to the world of pornography are now commonplace in family magazines and newspapers, in TV commercials, on billboards, online. Abercrombie & Fitch, a clothing store enormously popular with preteens and young teens, mails out catalogues and decorates its stores with photographs featuring nude and seminude teenagers in a variety of sexy poses and positions, including in threesomes. An international clothing chain store popular with young people is called f.c.u.k. "You can learn more about anatomy after school," says an ad featuring a young couple embracing in a school yard, an ad that manages to trivialize sex, relationships, and education all in one sentence. An ad for the Chuck Taylor line of Converse sneakers features a young couple pressed up against each other, his hands grasping her buttocks. "Get Chucked," says the copy in huge red letters. The ad for an energy drink called "Pimp Juice" states, "PJ is your mojo, your 'It' factor that works with women of every color, creed, or kind from 50 down to 9." These ads are aimed at tweens and teens, but very young children are exposed to them too, of course.

We and our children are awash in images of flawlessly beautiful and very young women in various states of undress, of men showing off their six-pack abs, and of perfect young couples imitating just about every form of copulation. These images define what is sexy and, more important, who is sexy. Women are portrayed as sexually desirable only if they are young, thin, carefully polished and groomed, made up, depilated, sprayed, and scented—rendered quite inhuman, in fact—and men are conditioned to seek such partners and to feel disappointed if they fail. Of course, men are increasingly objictified themselves in ads these days, although not nearly as often or with the same consequences as women.

People in ads are sexy because of the products they use, not because of who they are. The jeans, the perfume, the cars are sexy in and of themselves. The point is not to arouse desire for the person, but to arouse desire for the product. An ad for Gucci that ran in *Vogue* and other upscale women's magazines features a young man kneeling in front of a young woman. We see her only from the neck down. Her panties are lowered to reveal that her pubic hair is shaved into the shape of the Gucci logo. He is on his knees before her, worshipping Gucci. Things become lovers and lovers become things—perfect training for casual sex.

Alcohol advertising often encourages using alcohol to engage in impersonal sexual activity. "Names optional," says a beer ad featuring a man pressed against a woman, his hand covering her breast. This ad clearly suggests a sexual encounter so casual and fleeting that names don't need to be exchanged. Countless alcohol ads suggest to boys and young men that alcohol will help them seduce women and will make them great lovers (an ironic promise, given the relationship of alcohol to sexual dysfunction).

At the same time, girls and young women are offered alcohol as a way to escape the straitjacket of the double standard. "Be at least capable of bad," says an ad for cognac that features a very sultry young woman, and an ad for rum uses the slogan "Bad girls make good company." A recent Bud Light commercial shows an attractive young woman pouring a beer onto a man, then ripping off his shirt and licking the beer off his chest while he stands there, passive, befuddled. He is also pleased, of course, because boys and men have gotten the message from a very early age that they are always supposed to welcome sex, to be up for anything (as long as the woman is attractive). The woman's sexy female companions egg her on.

Fashion

When thongs and belly-baring shirts are marketed to seven-year-olds, it's hard to imagine what's left for older girls and teens. More of the same, it turns out. In recent years pornography has become increasingly mainstream, and we certainly see its influence in fashion. Clothing that used to be worn by strippers (albeit briefly!) is now on sale at the mall. Probably no article of clothing is more identified with strippers than the thong. And the sale of them to teenage girls is a lucrative business. In 2003, girls between the ages of thirteen and seventeen spent $152 million on thongs. One of the thongs sold by Delia's, a mall store popular with tweens and very young teens, has a four-leaf clover stamped on the front along with the words "Feeling lucky?" Parents complain to us all the time that it is difficult to find clothing for their tween and teen girls that is fashionable enough without making them look like hookers.

Fashion has long been used as a social weapon by teenage girls, but this is becoming more and more intense as fashion designers target tweens and teens. As brands are highlighted in TV shows and teen magazines, specific brands become ever more important to teenagers. In one study, more than one-third of middle-school students said they were bullied because of the clothes they wear. Although the prevalence of "fashion bullying" is greater in affluent cities and towns, it also exists in poorer communities.

Films

Adolescents make up the largest demographic segment of moviegoers, and increasing numbers of movies with sexual themes appear to be targeted specifically to them. As in other forms of media, the sexual messages in films are becoming more graphic and extreme. One movie critic, writing about *American Pie* (a 1999 film about four male high school seniors who are struggling to lose their virginity, a film so popular it spawned two sequels), noted that the film "is pitched to the first generation of male and female adolescents who have been taught, from birth . . . to act as sex objects for each other." A shocking idea then, this is commonplace now. In the prizewinning 2004 film *Me and You and Everyone We Know*, a barely pubescent boy is seduced into oral sex by two girls perhaps a year older, and his six-year-old brother logs on to a pornographic chat room and solicits a grown woman with instant messages about "poop."

The Internet

The Internet has made pornography instantly available to everyone, including children, erasing the barriers between porn and mainstream culture. As you read in Chapter 1, some children get their initial exposure to sex by accidentally stumbling onto porn sites. Young people don't have to go to "adult" bookstores in seedy parts of town or ask for magazines wrapped in plastic from behind a counter. Everything is available now in the privacy of one's own home—or anywhere over the phone or on one's handheld computer. Twelve percent of all websites are pornography sites, and 25 percent of all search engine requests are for pornography.

Far from being considered shameful or embarrassing, porn has become cool, edgy. Pimps, once seen as the losers and exploiters they are, now inspire Halloween costumes and Oscar-winning movie songs. Lauren Phoenix, star of scores of porn films such as *Anal Delinquents* and *Full Throttle Anal*, sells tube socks to teens in American Apparel ads, and porn queen Jenna Jameson has launched her own fashion line.

This contributes to the pornographic attitude toward sex, especially toward women, that dominates our culture these days. "The Internet gives teen boys the idea that girls are interchangeable sexual objects at their disposal," says Lynn Ponton, author of *The Sex Lives of Teenagers*. "So how can they ever be developmentally ready for a real-life relationship?"

Chat rooms and sites like MySpace, Facebook, and YouTube invite young people to put personal information and photographs on the Internet, thus giving precious information to marketers and exposing themselves to networks of strangers, as well as objectifying themselves to their friends and acquaintances (and to themselves). Children and teens often imitate the sexy poses of celebrities in these photos, posing in their underwear and flashing for the camera. A popular Facebook group called "Thirty Reasons Girls Should Call It a Night" shows young women passing out, vomiting, urinating in public, and drunkenly carousing. MySpace, a site for tweens and young teens, recently reported that it had identified and removed twenty-nine thousand convicted sex offenders caught using the site.

Magazines

Magazines targeting girls and young women are filled with ads and articles on how to be beautiful and sexy and appealing to boys—all in the service of advertisers, of course, who sell their wares on almost every page. "How Smart Girls Flirt," "Sex to Write Home About," "15 Ways Sex Makes You Prettier," "5 *Hot!* New Kisses (Try Them Tonight!)," "The Sex Position He Craves," and "A Shocking Thing 68% of Chicks Do in Bed" are some of the cover stories for recent issues of magazines popular with teenage girls.

Teenage boys read magazines far less often than their female peers. Certainly when boys read the "men's magazines" such as *Playboy* and *Maxim* or pore over the swimsuit issue of *Sports Illustrated*, they get very negative and sexist messages about women and very limited and stereotypical models of masculinity. One study of twenty-one covers of popular young women's magazines showed that 78 percent contained messages about physical appearance. None of the young men's magazine covers contained such messages.

Music

Some of us who remember fighting with our parents about the Rolling Stones or, further back, Elvis Presley may think that the more things change, the more they stay the same. The older generation never likes the music of the younger generation, so why so much fuss now? Well, there's a world of difference between Elvis shaking his hips and the Stones singing about Brown Sugar—and Ludacris rapping, "That's the way you like to fuck . . . rough sex make it hurt," or Eamon singing, "Fuck you, you ho, I don't want you back," or 50 Cent rapping, "I tell the hos all the time, / Bitch get in my car." These songs make "I Want to Hold Your Hand" seem like "The Wheels on the Bus."

Music plays a bigger role in the lives of tweens and teens than it does with younger children. Although it is sometimes creative and compelling, all too often it is also a very powerful source of destructive messages about sex and relationships. One study of the effects of listening to popular music on sexual behavior found that 40 percent of the lyrics studied contained sexual content and 15 percent were sexually degrading. Most such lyrics were concentrated within the work of hip-hop and R&B artists. But Britney Spears, originally popular with little girls, sings lyrics (generally written for her by middle-aged men) such as these from "Toxic": "You're toxic / I'm slipping under . . . I'm addicted to you / Intoxicate me now." The music video for "Toxic" features Britney writhing on the floor. Although she is wearing a bodysuit sprinkled with diamonds, she appears to be naked.

Britney began her career on *The Mickey Mouse Club* in 1993, when she was twelve years old. In the video for her first hit record, "(Hit Me) Baby One More Time," released in 1998, she wears a schoolgirl uniform with her blouse open and sucks on a lollipop. Most of her fans were little girls and tweens, just getting hooked on sexy music and the celebrity culture. Like other stars popular with very young girls, Britney became sexier and edgier as she grew older, in an attempt to appeal to an older audience. She came out with "Toxic" in 2004. Three years later, in the music video for "Gimme More," she pole-dances in a bar or strip club, wearing very short shorts and fishnet stockings. It should come as no surprise that well-known directors of pornographic films have directed some of the music videos of popular young singers like Britney and Christina Aguilera. Sadly, Britney also self-destructed, as many sexualized girls do, but she had the misfortune to do it on an international stage.

Britney is tame, though, compared with Lil' Kim, who sings, "I'll do it anywhere, anyhow / I'm down for anything." In the old days even suggestive song lyrics were usually subtle enough to go over the heads of little kids who happened to be around. That's rarely the case these days.

There is often sexual violence in the music favored by teenagers, especially rap and hip-hop. Black women are especially degraded in these songs and videos—referred to as "hos" and treated with contempt. In "Lollipop," Snoop Dogg sings, "Ho get up out of my face unless you tryin' to fuck." In the video for Nelly's "Tip Drill," a man swipes his credit card between a woman's buttocks. And the video for "P.I.M.P." by 50 Cent shows two women being walked on leashes.

In the music video for "SexyBack," pop idol Justin Timberlake has simulated sex with a bra-clad woman on broken glass (shattered when he pulls her to him). He rips a pearl necklace off her during the act. The white rap artist Eminem sings in "Kim" (the name of his ex-wife), "Now bleed, bitch, bleed bleed, bitch, bleed, bleeeeeed!"

Television

Television is the best-studied medium. Two-thirds of young people ages eight to eighteen have TVs in their bedrooms, and two-thirds live in homes with cable TV, providing unsupervised access to sex talk and scenes, as well as extremely graphic violence. One in four American children lives in a home with five or more TVs. Two-thirds live in homes where the TV is usually on during meals, and half live in homes where the TV is left on most of the time, whether anyone is watching it or not.

The sexual content of TV is pervasive and increasing, as is the number of TV shows that have sexual content. Indeed, the number of sexual scenes on TV has nearly doubled since 1998. Seventy percent of all TV programs contain sexual content, with 34 percent depicting or implying sexual behavior. The typical teenage viewer, who watches an average of three to five hours of television a day, sees a minimum of two thousand sexual acts per year on television alone. Almost all of this sexual activity is consequence-free, no matter how unplanned and unsafe it might be, and much of it exploits women's bodies and glamorizes sexual violence.

Video Games

The vast majority of children and adolescents play video games, and games made both for home systems and for computers contain highly sexualized content and few strong female protagonists. Many of the most popular video games, such as *Grand Theft Auto,* which we described earlier, encourage sexual violence.

Although there is a video game rating system, it is implemented by the video game industry itself, not by an independent regulatory agency. Thus many games that have highly sexualized and violent content do not receive the AO (Adults Only) rating. Many M-rated (Mature) video games are specifically marketed and deliberately sold to youths younger than seventeen.

THE IMPACT OF MEDIA MESSAGES ON TEENAGERS

Young people today spend an average of nearly six and a half hours a day using media. Yet there is actually very little scientific research on the impact of the media—on violence, on consumerism, on sexual attitudes and behavior, or anything else.

There are several reasons for this. First, it is difficult to find a comparison group, a group that hasn't been exposed to massive doses of the same or similar media messages. Second, the changes in the culture have been quite rapid, and it takes a while for research to catch up. Perhaps most important, the most extensive research projects require a lot of money and are usually funded by industries that hope to benefit from the information obtained. Often these potential donors don't want the public to have this information. Why would they want to give money to research projects that could provide the public with information that might diminish their profits or their reputations?

It is particularly difficult to do research on the sexual attitudes and behavior of young people because of the sensitivity of the topic, especially in a conservative political climate. Almost no research has been done on the impact of the sexualized popular culture on younger children. It has infiltrated childhood in recent years with very little recognition of its possible impact until recently, and researchers have only begun to think about how to study it. There hasn't been very much research on teenagers either. The few studies that do exist consistently point to a relationship between exposure to sexual content in the media and sexual beliefs, attitudes, and behavior.

In general, key communications theories and years of research on other kinds of communications effects, such as the effect of violent images, suggest that young people are indeed affected by the ubiquitous, graphic, and consequence-free depictions of sexual behavior that surround them in all forms of the mass media. Film, TV, music, and magazines have at least as much influence on teen sexual behavior as religion, parents, and peers. Heavy exposure to media alters a viewer's perception of social reality in a way that matches the media world. So although most of the messages about sex in the media are inaccurate, misleading, and distorted, young people generally accept them as fact, given the absence of accurate sex education in their lives.

Speaking of peers, the influence of peers on teenagers is well documented and accepted. Less well known, however, is that the media function as a kind of *super peer,* often even more influential with teens than their parents or friends. Most children and teenagers are sensitive to peer pressure and find it difficult to resist or even to question the dominant cultural messages perpetuated and reinforced by the media. The media's and marketers' efforts to create a strong peer culture while deliberately undermining the influence of caring adults begin with little children and intensify as children grow older. Mass communication has made possible a kind of national peer pressure that erodes private and individual values and standards, as well as those of families and communities.

One study found that three out of four fifteen- to seventeen-year-olds indicated that sexual content on TV influences the behavior of their peers "somewhat" or "a lot." Given the reluctance of most teenagers to admit to being anything other than completely independent, it is not surprising that only one in four thought TV influenced their own behavior! However, another survey of teenagers found that they believed that TV "encouraged" them—even more than their friends did—to have sex. In a survey of more than two thousand teenage girls, only eleven-year-olds said that they do not feel pressure from the media to have sex.

None of this should come as a surprise. As pediatrician and media expert Victor Strasburger says, "In any given society, at any given moment in history, people become sexual the same way they become anything else. Without much reflection, they pick up directions from their social environment. . . . For teenagers, who are eager to soak up any available information that is related to sex and sexuality, the media offer 'scripts' in which gender roles, courtship, and sexual gratification are modeled recurrently. . . . Children and teens learn behavior by observing others, directly in real life and vicariously, through the media." What are our teenagers learning from the media and the popular culture these days? And how do these lessons influence their behavior?

Mass Media as Sex Education

University of North Carolina researcher Jane Brown and her colleagues concluded from their many years of research that the mass media are important sex educators for American teenagers. The average American teenager views nearly fourteen thousand sexual references in the media every year. Brown found that white adolescents who chose media with a lot of sexual content when they were ages twelve to fourteen were twice as likely as the other young people in the study to have had sex by age sixteen. She found that black teens are more influenced by parental expectations and peer behavior. Other potential educators, such as parents, schools, and churches, are doing an inadequate job and, even if that were to change dramatically, the media and commercial culture would remain compelling teachers. As Brown said, "If you believe *Sesame Street* taught your four-year-old something, then you better believe MTV is teaching your fourteen-year-old something, because the influence doesn't stop when we come to a certain age."

Two studies with older children have found correlations between watching higher doses of "sexy" television and early initiation of sexual intercourse, and studies of adolescents have found that heavy television viewing is predictive of negative attitudes toward virginity. A study by the Rand Corporation found that teenagers who listen to sexually degrading music lyrics are nearly twice as likely to have sex within two years as teens who listen to other types of music. This was true for boys and girls, regardless of race. Another study found that young black girls who frequently watched rap music videos were more likely to binge drink, have sex with multiple partners, and have a negative body image.

Dr. Brown faults media portrayals for avoiding the "three C's"— commitment, contraceptives, and consequences—and concludes, "it is little wonder that adolescents find the sexual world a difficult and often confusing place and that they engage in early and unprotected sexual intercourse with multiple partners." As we show throughout this book, however, looking at the impact of media on teenagers alone ignores the fact that the foundations for teenage sexual behavior are laid in childhood. And, as we said, there is even less research on how children are affected by the media.

Although graphic sexual messages abound in the media, there is rarely any accurate information about sex (the major networks still refuse to run condom ads) and certainly never any emphasis on relationships or intimacy. To make matters worse, we have to fight to get any sort of sex education into our schools, let alone the kinds of broad-based program that could help to counteract the disturbing lessons children are getting from the popular culture (such as Connie's program, which we discussed in Chapter 6).

Although the sexual sell, overt and subliminal, is at a fever pitch throughout all forms of the media, depictions of sex as an important and potentially profound human activity are notably absent. Couples in ads rarely look at each other. Men and women in music videos use each other. It is a cold and oddly passionless sex that surrounds us. A sense of joy is also absent; the people involved often look either hostile or bored. The real obscenity is the reduction of people to objects. Our culture is sex-crazed and sex-saturated, but strangely not erotic. As French philosopher Roland Barthes said, speaking of Japan, "Sexuality is in sex, not elsewhere; in the United States, it is the contrary; sex is everywhere, except in sexuality."

Of course, all these sexual images aren't intended to sell our children or us on sex—they are intended to sell us on shopping. The desire they want to inculcate is not for orgasm but for more gizmos. This is the intent of the marketers—but an unintended consequence is the effect these images have on real sexual desire and real lives. When sex is a commodity, there is always a better deal. The wreckage that ensues when people (young and old) try to emulate the kind of sexuality glorified in the ads and the popular culture is everywhere. We certainly see it in the lives of many of our teenagers.

Hooking Up

It's not news that a lot of teenagers are having sex these days. Teenagers have always had sex. Roughly half of all fifteen- to nineteen-year-olds have had vaginal intercourse, and more than half have had oral sex. What's new is the kind of sex many of these young people are having—a casual and impersonal kind of sex. Some teenagers engage in serial sex, without affection, indeed without emotion. They refer to these encounters as "hooking up" and having "friends with benefits."

When young people treat their sexual partners as objects rather than engaging in sex connected to caring relationships, they not only put themselves at physical risk, they lose the precious opportunity to practice the skills that are necessary to make an intimate relationship work later on. Robbed of the chance to gradually become intimate, to learn about relationships, how can young people learn to have constructive conflict and solve the problems that inevitably arise in close relationships? They can end up like the twenty-two-year-old client of Seattle psychologist Laura Kastner: "She knows how to hang in bars, flirt, and go home with a hookup. She doesn't know how to spend time with a person, one on one. That scares her. She feels like a loser, she feels disconnected and empty, and has low self-esteem."

One male college student described the "hookup culture" as "a whirlwind of drunkenness and horniness that lacks definition—which is what everyone likes about it [because] it's just an environment of craziness and you don't have to worry about it until the next morning." But a female student on the same campus said, "I think the ease of hooking up has, like, made people forget what they truly want. People assume that there are two very distinct elements in a relationship, one emotional and one sexual, and they pretend like there are clean lines between them."

The Double Bind for Teenage Girls

These kinds of sexual experiences are harmful to most young people, but especially to girls. At least one study has found that teenage girls who use drugs or are sexually active are more likely to become clinically depressed later on. Researchers found that among girls, even modest involvement in drug use and sexual experimentation were predictors of future depression—raising their risk two- or threefold—but for boys, only frequent marijuana use and high-risk behavior like binge drinking appeared to raise the risk of depression.

It's not surprising there is such a gender difference here. In spite of all the graphic sexual messages in the media that urge girls and young women to be "hot" and sexy (starting at a very early age, as you have seen), there is still a powerful double standard, with very different rules and consequences for females and males. Girls are constantly told by the popular culture that they should be sexy but innocent, experienced but virginal. As many of us know, this is tricky!

At the same time they are learning how important it is to be *sexy,* girls still get the message—from many parents, from the abstinence-only sex education taught in schools, from almost every religion—that they must not be *sexual.* They get this message also from witnessing what happens to the girls and women who are sexual—the ones who get called "sluts" and "hos"—and the celebrities who self-destruct in the limelight, such as Britney Spears and Lindsay Lohan.

Females have long been categorized as either virgins or whores, of course. What is new is that girls are now supposed to embody *both* within themselves—and that even very little girls are encouraged to look sexy long before they have any real understanding of what this actually means. These conflicting messages put girls in an impossible double bind. No wonder so many teenage girls are depressed!

One way that some girls deal with the contradiction is to use alcohol, both to lessen their inhibitions and to numb their emotions. It is no coincidence that the hookup culture is a "whirlwind of drunkenness." A young woman can manage to have sex and yet in some sense maintain her virginity by being "out of control," drunk, and/or deep in denial about the entire experience. It is not surprising that most teenage pregnancies begin when one or both parties are drunk. Alcohol and other mind-altering drugs permit sexual activity at the same time that they allow denial. One is almost literally not there. The next day one has an excuse: I was drunk. I was swept away. I did not choose this experience.

Girls who want to be sexually *active* instead of simply being the objects of male desire are given only one model to follow in the media, that of exploitive male sexuality. It seems that the popular culture can't conceive of a kind of power that isn't manipulative and exploitive or a way that a woman can be actively sexual without being like a traditional man. So, for all the attention paid to girls in recent years, what girls are offered mostly by the popular culture is a superficial toughness, an "attitude," exemplified in childhood by the Bratz dolls and the posturing of some of the singers popular with very young girls (such as Britney Spears in the early stages of her career) and in adolescence by smoking, drinking, and engaging in casual sex.

You may be surprised to hear this, but the model in the popular culture of desirable female sexuality today comes straight from pornography. Paris Hilton's sex video makes her famous. Porn stars and call girls write bestsellers. From a young age, girls are encouraged to dress and act like hookers and strippers—to remove all or almost all of their pubic hair (via "Brazilian" waxes), to wear G-strings (now called "thongs"), to pole-dance at parties and make out with other girls in order to titillate boys. Even girls as young as six-year-old Sasha know how to do a "sexy" dance.

Young women are active participants in this culture, to be sure. Indeed, it couldn't exist without them. They attend parties on college campuses with themes such as "Dress to Get Lei'd," "Presidents and Interns," "Give It to Me, Daddy, I Want It," and "Pimpin' All Over the World." College students willingly flash their breasts to be part of "Girls Gone Wild," a $100 million entertainment empire based on amateur videotapes. And many young women put up with impersonal sex and disrespectful treatment (and worse) from men.

Some make the terrible mistake of believing that being seen as sex objects, dressing up as male fantasies, and having meaningless sexual encounters is empowering and liberating. These women confuse erotic power with actual power in the real world. As one female college student said, "It's kind of like domination through sex." Donna Lisker, director of Duke University's women's center, sees it differently, however. She says, "They've gotten this message from the media and other places that part of being a modern woman is sort of playing with your sexuality. . . . They think at this party that they're exercising control. They think that they're showing these boys how it's done by pouring grain alcohol down their throats, by dressing in a sexy way. What they don't necessarily get is that you put on that Playboy-bunny outfit and you're stepping into a history of objectification."

The "bad girls" often end up suffering real-world consequences because of the double standard. Eight students were suspended from a Virginia high school not long ago—three boys and two girls for engaging in oral sex and intercourse on school property and three other boys for watching. Afterward their schoolmates called the girls involved "sluts" and "whores," but criticized the boys only for jeopardizing the football team. There is still no pejorative equivalent to "slut" for a man. As columnist Maureen Dowd said, "Men are players, women are sluts, just the way men are tough and women are bitchy."

Self-Image and Body Image

Even if girls repeatedly get the message from the popular culture that emulating the sexualized models presented by the media and other cultural sources brings them power, research shows otherwise. The *Report of the APA* (American Psychological Association) *Task Force on the Sexualization of Girls*, referred to in earlier chapters, reviewed over three hundred studies and concluded that exposure to sexualized images, lyrics, fashion, role models, and other pop-culture influences made girls think of and treat their own bodies as sexual objects. Other research has found that this self-objectification, this tendency to view one's physical self as if one were an outside observer, has a host of negative emotional consequences, such as depression, shame, and anxiety. It can contribute to physical consequences as well, such as eating disorders and self-mutilation. It can also lead to feelings of disgust about one's body. Indeed, hating one's body is *normal* for teenage girls these days (and for many grown women as well)—and is increasingly normal for little girls.

Many studies link media usage by teenage girls with disordered body image. A study of ninth-grade girls found that their music video consumption correlated with their concerns about their appearance and their weight. Another found that watching music videos of girl bands, such as Sugababes and the Pussycat Dolls, even very briefly, can be as detrimental as seeing models in magazines. And yet another study found that girls ages nine to fourteen who said that they wanted to look like television or movie stars were twice as likely to be concerned about their weight, to be constant dieters, and to engage in purging behavior. Fashion magazines for teen girls can be particularly unhealthy. More than two-thirds of girls in fifth through twelfth grades report that their ideal body shape is influenced by the fashion magazines they read. And we all know how incredibly skinny the models and celebrities featured in fashion magazines are these days.

Although it is unfortunately beyond the scope of this book to address the differences for young women of different races, ethnic groups, socioeconomic levels, and levels of ability, it is clear that the messages about body image in the media for women of color are more complex. Although larger body types are acceptable, and even seen as desirable, in the African American and Latino communities, women in these groups are not immune to the obsession with thinness or to eating disorders. The body type most desirable in these communities— that of a woman with large buttocks and thighs but thin elsewhere—is as impossible to attain as is the stick-thin body type (but with large breasts) seen as desirable for white women. African American women may be protected from a preoccupation with thinness and dieting, but they are often at risk for obesity, which has its own set of problems. Girls with physical disabilities have their own challenges, of course, in developing a healthy self-image and sexuality in a culture that is contemptuous of everything short of perfection in women's appearance.

The pressure on young women to attain an ideal (and impossible) image of beauty is becoming steadily worse. Several studies have found that young women today feel tremendous pressure to be *perfect*. They feel they have to have perfect hair, skin, and clothes and also to be extremely thin—as well as to be "hot" and sexy and to excel academically. They also feel they mustn't be perceived as trying too hard, but must create an illusion of *effortless perfection*.

Some experts believe there is a link between the increasing pressure on girls to be sexy, thin, and "perfect" and the increasing rates of depression and suicide among girls and young women. Girls are twice as likely as boys to experience a major depressive episode by the age of fifteen, placing them at increased risk of suicide. Between 2003 and 2004 the suicide rate for girls ages ten to fourteen jumped 76 percent. The single group of teenagers most likely to consider suicide are girls who think they are overweight.

As this pressure has steadily increased, we increasingly witness its impact on young women's sense of themselves and their sexuality and on their relationships with men. Women who have been conditioned all their lives to feel that their value depends mostly on their physical attractiveness and desirability to men and who measure themselves against an impossible standard are bound to feel anxious and insecure. And, no matter how much they flaunt their sexuality, they are unlikely to feel very sexy. How sexy can a woman truly be who hates her body? A girl who has negative feelings about her body in adolescence is likely to focus more on her partner's judgment of her than on her own desires, pleasure, and safety (which can interfere with practicing safer sex). And she may well have sexual problems in adulthood too.

Girls lose in other ways as well. Those who are preoccupied with appearance have less time and energy to devote to other pursuits. This can affect their performance in school and limit their options for the future. This preoccupation can also affect their relationships with other girls, leading them to be more competitive for the attention of boys and less supportive of one another. The "mean girls" we've read so much about in recent years usually attack other girls on the basis of appearance and sexual behavior.

Sexual Violence

The popular culture not only objectifies women and trivializes sex, it also often links sex with violence—with dreadful consequences. Media violence has not only increased in quantity in recent years—it has also become more graphic, sexual, and sadistic. Quite a few young men have learned to associate sex with domination and violence.

Nearly half of American high school students have had sexual intercourse. Of these, a little over 7 percent report having sex before the age of thirteen, and 14 percent have had more than four partners. These are disturbing facts. Far more disturbing, however, is the fact that seven in ten girls who had sex before the age of fourteen, and six in ten of those who had sex before the age of fifteen, report having sex involuntarily. Nine out of ten girls ages fifteen to seventeen report feeling "some" or "a lot of" pressure about sex. These terrible facts illustrate how little sexual power many girls have.

Some girls and young women give in to sexual pressure and accept boorish behavior because they are afraid of losing their partners if they don't. Others are afraid of arousing anger. Forty-one percent of the teenage girls (ages fourteen to seventeen) in one study had had unwanted sex at some point. The most common reason was fear that their boyfriend would get angry. Ten percent were forced to have sex—in other words, they were raped—by their "boyfriends."

National research suggests that one in five high school girls is physically or sexually abused by a dating partner and nearly one in three experiences some type of abuse (physical, sexual, or psychological) in her dating relationships.

The seeds of this sexual violence are sown in childhood. As you read in Chapter 3, children don't really understand what sex is or what "sexy" means. Sasha and Tessa and other little girls who want to be sexy learn to present themselves in a certain way without understanding the ramifications. They also learn to see themselves as passive and powerless. These girls are completely unprepared for what happens when they reach adolescence and some boys, emerging from their own sexualized childhoods—their exposure to pornography at an early age, and their immersion in a culture that equates masculinity with violence—demand that they *deliver the goods.*

Many studies have found that frequent exposure to media with highly sexualized imagery may lead to greater acceptance by both men and women of attitudes that sexually objectify women. For example, girls and young women who watch a lot of "reality" TV (shows that are especially popular with young people) are more likely to accept sexual stereotypes, including a double standard regarding sexual activity for men and women. Men who are frequent readers of men's magazines such as *Maxim* and *Sports Illustrated,* who accept media portrayals, and who watch TV to learn about the world are also more accepting of traditional masculine beliefs, including the sexual objectification of women. Not only are beliefs affected by exposure to sexualized content, but actual behavior is as well. Men exposed to sexualized content are more likely to treat women as sex objects.

Given the link between sexist beliefs and acceptance of violence against women, it is not surprising that this exposure can also lead to acceptance of rape myths (such as that women ask to be raped), sexual harassment and violence, and adversarial beliefs about sexual relationships. For both boys and girls ages eleven to sixteen, frequent TV viewing and greater exposure to R- and X-rated films were related to stronger acceptance of sexual harassment. And African American teenage girls exposed to sexualized rap videos are more accepting of teen dating violence than those not exposed.

As if all this weren't bad enough, it is also very likely that the sexualization of girls in the media contributes to the increase in child pornography, sex trafficking, and the sexual abuse of children. According to the APA report mentioned earlier, a "particularly pernicious effect of the constant exposure to sexualized images of girls is that individuals and society may be *trained* to perceive and label sexualized girls as *seductive*. Images of young girls who are made to look like adult women (such as many of the models in the fashion magazines) may evoke similar responses. These images may also contribute to the trafficking and prostitution of girls by helping to create a market for sex with children through the cultivation of new desires and experiences. If the idealized female sexual partner is a fifteen-year-old girl, male consumers may demand pornography featuring such girls and the opportunity to pay for sex with them."

The Cost to Teenage Boys and Men

Almost all of the research that has been done on the effects of sexualization focuses on girls. Without question, boys suffer too, although less overtly and in a different way. Boys who are socialized to repress their feelings, treat themselves and others as objects, and rely only on themselves often grow into men who experience a range of psychological and physiological problems. Boys who are taught to equate masculinity with violence cause a lot of problems for others but also do harm to themselves.

As you saw in Chapter 1, boys are learning to objectify girls and women at very young ages. Boys today are surrounded by media messages that encourage them to judge their female peers based on how they look, often to view them with contempt, and to expect sexual subservience from them. At the age of five, James watched the professional wrestling girls with his older brother. He was still sensitive and innocent enough to be troubled by the images, but what will happen to him as he grows older and becomes increasingly desensitized to similar images that surround him? Ten-year-old Gabe learned from the Internet that sex doesn't have to be linked with affection or emotion. He was lucky to have a teacher who challenged him to think more deeply about this. But will he be able to resist this message as he enters adolescence?

Young men these days are quite actively discouraged from entering into mutually satisfactory intimate and committed relationships with women. Men who have been conditioned to judge women by the current standard of beauty and to compare real women with the idealized images in the popular media and pornography often find it difficult, if not impossible, to feel empathy for women. Needless to say, they are unlikely to be satisfying partners for women. Boys who lack empathy, who have compassion deficit disorder, often become men who find it impossible to have deep and fulfilling intimate relationships with their partners, with their children, with anyone. This is a very high price to pay.

A 2008 study in *The Journal of Adolescence* found that, contrary to the stereotype of the teenage boy who has only sex on his mind (constantly reinforced by most movies aimed at teens), many teenage boys actually are motivated by love and a desire to form real relationships with girls. This should not be surprising. More and more research, including research on the brain, is attesting to the importance of attachment for all human beings, men as well as women.

Yet boys are still socialized in a way that makes attachment and intimacy more difficult to achieve. They are often encouraged to be invulnerable, tough, and uncommunicative (especially about feelings). Many boys witness or directly experience male violence in their own homes. Men who treat women badly are often portrayed as heroes, in real life and in the media. This is a kind of blueprint for disastrous relationships. Women are the obvious and immediate losers, but men lose too.

THE CLASH OF CULTURES INTENSIFIES

The conflict between the family culture and the commercial culture, the two different boxes in children's heads that we discussed in Chapter 4, becomes even more extreme for adolescents. Some of this has to do with the way the adolescent brain develops. To some extent adolescents need to define themselves as different from their parents, as unique and independent. One of the great ironies of adolescence, of course, is how dependent most teens are on their peers! And some of it has to do with a popular culture that alienates children from their parents. This clash of cultures becomes more intense and more dangerous as children enter adolescence and as parents have less and less control.

If children have been through the premature adolescent rebellion described in Chapter 1 at the age of seven, what's left for them to rebel against when they hit thirteen? If they are having experiences at age eight or nine that used to occur in adolescence, if they are dressing like teenagers and sharing the same media, how can they not be bored and jaded and looking for new thrills when they finally become adolescents?

In the past, the prevailing cultural messages were more compatible with the values and goals that most parents held for their children. As George Gerbner, one of the world's most respected researchers on the influence of the media, said, "For the first time in human history, most of the stories about people, life, and values are told not by parents, schools, churches, or others in the community who have something to tell, but by a group of distant conglomerates that have something to sell."

Today there is grave disconnection between the values caring parents want to convey to their children about relationships, sex, and sexuality and the messages conveyed by the popular culture. Many parents feel they need to fight the current cultural messages at every turn with younger and younger children. Even the best-prepared and most conscientious parents find it impossible to stem the onslaught of negative media and marketing messages. They feel helpless to fight the power of a multibillion-dollar industry that uses state-of-the-art knowledge of psychology and marketing strategies to reel children in and exploit their vulnerabilities. As cultural anthropologist Margaret Mead once said, "Today our children are not brought up by parents, they are brought up by the mass media."

It can be very difficult for parents to understand how different the world is for their teenagers from the one they grew up in. There are similarities, to be sure—the self-absorption, the drama, the anxiety and insecurity, the need to be liked and to be popular, the conformity, the raging hormones. But this is all playing out on a new and unfamiliar stage. The sexual arena for young people these days is in many ways as different from that of the past as the cell phone is different from the rotary dial and party line of the good old days, as different as the Internet from the Pony Express. However, as we said earlier, don't despair! In the next two chapters we'll look at some of the ways that parents can make a powerful difference.

Chapter 8

Helping Teenagers
Through the Minefields

In Chapter 5 we provided guidelines and strategies for helping your children navigate the sexualized culture. In this chapter we discuss how these guidelines can be used to help teenagers. As we said earlier, this is not an exhaustive list, and the guidelines are not mutually exclusive. There are many resources at the end of this book that provide much more detailed information about teens.

THE GUIDELINES

1. Protect children as much as possible from exposure to sexual imagery and related content in the media and popular culture.

Of course, parents of teenagers have much less control over what *their* children are exposed to and do. But that doesn't mean you have no control or influence! With tweens and young teens you can still negotiate rules about what is considered appropriate in your family. As researcher Kate Rademacher says, "Just as we help our children to eat healthy food, we must help them learn to make healthy choices about how much and what types of media they consume."

To begin with, it's almost always a bad idea to allow computers and television sets in children's bedrooms. Nonetheless, nearly two-thirds of teenagers say they have a TV in their bedroom, and most say their parents have no idea what they are watching. If at all possible, have your children use their computers in family areas where you can occasionally glance over their shoulders. Let your young teens know that you will check the history of websites they visit. Even with older children, you can help them be selective about what they listen to and watch.

It probably goes without saying that you should make every effort not to buy inappropriate clothing, games, CDs, DVDs, and other media for your children. If your older teens insist, try to find a solution or compromise using the give-and-take conversation style we've discussed.

Encourage your children to engage in other activities—a sport, a passion such as drama or music or science, a spiritual practice, yoga, meditation, social or political activism. These are important alternatives to the values of the consumer culture. Of course, as always, it is also important for you to model this by limiting your own consumption and television watching and by engaging in other activities yourself!

2. Learn about the media and popular culture in your child's life—popular TV programs, movies, video and computer games, fashion, celebrities.

We can help our children become media-literate, both by fighting for media literacy programs in our schools and by talking with them about the media. Studies show that parents' views can override depictions in the media, but only if the parent is watching the same show as the teen and actually expresses an opinion.

When Jean's daughter, Claudia, was in elementary school, Jean used to look at the television schedule every week and select a few programs to record. She and Claudia then watched them together and talked about them. It is more difficult to do this with teenagers, but you can still go to the movies with them and watch the occasional TV show. Some parents and teens have a show or two that they watch together regularly. Digital video recorders (DVRs) make this easy.

If you know your teenagers are watching programs outside of the home that you don't want them to see (and they are!), it is still important to talk with them and respectfully exchange opinions.

Be aware of other media that your teenagers are using. Let them teach you about them. Listen to their music and play their video games and talk with them, being careful never to condemn the media they love or blame them for loving them. Help them (and yourself!) become more critical viewers and listeners. Ask a lot of questions, listen to the responses, and then express your own opinions.

Most likely your teen is using the social network site MySpace or Facebook (the site for older teens). It's a good idea to join these sites yourself so you can get a sense of what is going on. With your young teens you can and should set clear limits and boundaries regarding whom they correspond with and the content of photos and messages. It is also important to ask them to tell you if someone they encounter online seems strange or creepy. Pedophiles do lurk on these sites, pretending to be teenagers, and sometimes succeed in enticing naïve teens to meet them. Teach your kids never to give out personal information online.

Check out YouTube (an extremely popular online site where people contribute their own homemade videos on an extremely wide variety of topics). Your children most likely are regular visitors to the site. Some of the content is very creative and funny and can be shared and enjoyed with your children.

Encourage your child to critique the media and the popular culture—to speak out, to protest, to write zines and blogs, to develop alternatives.

3. Get beyond the "Just say no" approach.

Be as aware as possible of what is really going on in your teenagers' world—with your children and with their friends. Most parents don't really know very much about their teen's sexual behavior. Share your values and your expectations with your teen. If you disapprove of teens' being sexually active, say so and give your reasons why.

Common sense tells us that it's important to talk honestly with our children, and the research bears that out. University of North Carolina researcher Jane Brown and her colleagues found that one of the strongest protective factors against early sexual behavior was clear parental communication about sex. Teenagers who reported their parents did not want them to have sex were less likely to have engaged in sexual intercourse by the time they were sixteen years old than those who perceived less parental disapproval of teen sex.

Of course, sexual activity is different from all the other risky behaviors that attract our teens. Although most of us want our children to delay having sex until they are old enough to be responsible and until they are in a loving relationship (for some parents this means marriage, but certainly not for all), we want them eventually to have happy and healthy sex lives—just not when they are thirteen! It is the corporate exploitation of our children's sexuality that is disgusting and dangerous, not the sexuality itself. As researcher and pediatrician Victor Strasburger says, when it comes to helping our teens deal with sex and sexuality, "Just say no" is not a very useful message (for drugs either, but that's another story). "Just say 'later' " is probably more accurate for most of us. We want our teens to experience the joy of blossoming sexuality and passion while avoiding the pitfalls of a culture in which all too often people are objects and sex is just another kind of consuming.

4. Establish safe channels for talking about sexual development and related issues with your children.

If you have done this when your kids were young, it will not be difficult to continue the conversations with your teenager. If you haven't done this, however, it is never too late to begin! You might even say that you are sorry you didn't begin these conversations sooner, but that you'd really like to now.

Just as with the advice we gave you for talking with younger children, if you want your teens to talk to you, you need to be willing to listen and not rush in with judgments or advice or even sympathy. Sometimes a simple nod is the right response. Allow them to voice their opinions and make their own decisions (because they will anyway, whether you know about it or not). If you respect them and encourage them to respect themselves, they will make more responsible and healthier choices. As always, communication is the key.

5. *Make age-appropriate give-and-take conversations about the sexualization of childhood issues an essential part of your relationship with your child.*

As with younger children, don't worry about having the perfect answer, the right response. If you don't know the answer to a question your teen asks, don't be afraid to say so. Suggest that you research it together. The important thing is to have an ongoing conversation. Be sure to tell your children that they can ask you anything—don't assume that they know that.

6. *Help your teenagers process the sexual images and other media messages they see.*

Ask questions about what they are seeing and how they feel about it. Don't jump right in with your own opinion. Encourage critical analysis. Many of the organizations in our Resources section (such as the American Academy of Pediatrics) have tip sheets and advice for parents about talking with teens about media messages. CMCH (the Center on Media and Child Health) provides up-to-date research, newsletters, a monthly column for parents, and a search engine that will answer questions on a wide variety of topics.

7. *Work to counteract the negative impact of the narrow gender stereotypes that are so prominent in the media and the commercial culture.*

One of the best ways to do this is to challenge the assumptions about gender that surround us. Ask your daughter to help you repair something. Ask your son to help cook and clean up. Encourage a broad range of interests and skills in your child, regardless of gender. Focus on what your children do, on important qualities such as compassion, kindness, perseverance, rather than on how they look (but tell them they look good, too, of course!). Be a role model yourself and point out examples of positive male and female role models—in your family, your community, the wider world.

Avoid sexist comments yourself, and remark on ones you hear from your teens. "What makes you think that?" or "Funny you should say that about women. It isn't true of me—or of your sister," or "Do you really think that's true of all men? How about your Uncle David?" Ask them how they feel about a woman being called a "ho" in popular music—or a man being called a "pussy" or a "wimp" if he expresses emotion. Point out the contempt for women and the homophobia behind these words. Bring these attitudes into consciousness, into the light.

Support media that promote positive images of males and females—shows, products, music, magazines, even some ad campaigns. You can find some examples on the Internet, as well as on our Resources list. For example, a group of girls and young women in New York have formed a group that analyzes mainstream ad campaigns aimed at girls and works to create better ads and media. The group is called "3iying" and can be found on YouTube as well as their own website, 3iying.com. There are many groups and programs these days, such as "Hardy Girls Healthy Women" and "Turn Beauty Inside Out," that encourage girls to form coalitions and to examine the messages they get from the media about looks, bodies, and clothing.

8. *Counteract compassion deficit disorder by helping teenagers learn how to have positive and caring relationships.*

Above all, model healthy intimate relationships for your children. Of course, don't abuse other people or tolerate abuse yourself (including from your children!). Be physically affectionate with your children (insofar as they'll allow it!). Let your children know that conflict is inevitable in close relationships and teach them ways to resolve conflict peacefully. The best way to teach this is to model it in your relationships with them and with others.

9. *When conflicts arise between you and your child about sexuality and related issues, try to come up with a mutually agreeable solution.*

Talk about disagreements. Consider different points of view. Try to compromise whenever possible. Also choose your battles carefully. Be adamant on issues of health and safety, but don't worry about giving ground on other less important issues. For example, Jean let her daughter get her navel pierced (and went with her to be sure it was done properly), but drew the line at tattoos (because of their permanence). Try not to take everything personally (we know that's difficult!).

Diane and her husband, Gary, worked out a successful strategy with their son Eli when he was a teenager and getting involved in more independent and sometimes risky activities. They made a deal that Eli would tell them the truth about anything he wanted to do and that Diane and Gary would do their best to allow it, if they could find a way for him to do it that felt *safe*. They rated every situation with a number—#1 meant yes (it's safe), #2 meant maybe (if we can talk it through and come up with a way for it to be safe), and #3 meant no (we can't come up with a way to make it feel safe). One time Eli and a group of his friends wanted to go to a friend's house after a high school prom. But he knew the friend's parents would not be there and would not know about the party. This did not feel safe to Diane and Gary. They rated it a clear #3 and were able to convey their concerns in a long conversation with Eli. Diane and Gary were then torn between a wish to let the friend's parents know of the plan, which would violate Eli's trust, and fear that something bad might happen in this unsafe situation. They discussed this concern with Eli. Eventually Eli talked to his friend, who ended up telling his parents about the party. They agreed that the parents would stay on call at the house next door and would check in a couple of times during the event. Such discussions helped Eli arrive at a better understanding of risks and an increasing ability to figure them out on his own (one of our goals with our kids, after all!).

10. *Share your values and concerns with other caring adults—relatives, and the parents of your children's friends.*

Insofar as possible, get to know the parents of your children's friends. It can be enormously helpful to share the trials and tribulations (and the joys) of living with a teenager. You can gain perspective on your own experience and get a sense of whether you are being too strict or too lenient with your teen. It can also increase your sense of safety to know where your teen is hanging out. If your teen is going to a party, call ahead (whether you know the parents or not) to be sure an adult will be present. Your child may say you are the only parent in the universe who does this, but it won't be true!

Another important part of connecting with your teens is getting to know their friends. If at all possible, make your home Teen Central. Most teenagers don't care if a home is huge or luxurious—it just needs to be warm and welcoming and comfortable. We both found it exhilarating to have young people around, and we learned a lot from the conversations (both the ones we took part in and the ones we overheard!). When Diane's son Eli was a teenager, he hung out with friends in the basement of her house while she worked at a table in the kitchen. Everyone had to go through the kitchen to get to the basement. The little chats that resulted each time they passed through provided a wonderful opportunity for Diane and the teens to get to know one another.

We're sure it goes without saying that there should always be an adult present when teens have their friends over. But the adult doesn't have to hover!

11. Ask your child's school to take seriously its vital role in working with children and families to counteract the harm caused by the sexualization of childhood.

Middle schools and high schools should be teaching accurate, age-appropriate sex education. They should also be teaching students to be media-literate. And they should be working to prevent bullying and sexual harassment. This means we need to elect politicians who will place a priority on the well-being of young people and who will give schools the resources they need. We'll discuss this further in the next chapter.

STAYING CONNECTED WITH YOUR TEENAGER

One fact that can seem funny to almost everyone who isn't the parent of a teenager is that many surveys have found that half the parents who say their kids are not sexually experienced are wrong. In one study, 58 percent of middle school students attending an adolescent clinic were sexually active, but 98 percent of their parents thought otherwise. This is sad too, of course, because it illustrates a painful lack of authentic communication between parents and teens.

Talking with children about sex has always been harder for most parents than talking about other complex issues, such as poverty, violence, or illness. Many adults struggle to talk openly and comfortably about sex and sexuality with one another, let alone with children, and the task becomes even more daunting in the current context. Some parents, feeling helpless to stem the tide of graphic sexual content in their children's lives, deal with the discomfort by denying the potential harm or doubting their ability to have a positive influence. This leaves children even more vulnerable.

Not surprisingly, every reasonable book on parenting a teenager (or being in any other kind of relationship, for that matter) stresses the importance of communication. Children whose parents don't talk with them about sex and intimate relationships are at the mercy of the media and the marketers—with their incessant messages about sex as casual, fun, risk-free. It should be abundantly clear to you by now that the people crafting these messages do not have our children's best interests at heart.

As parents, the most important thing we can do for our children is to connect deeply and honestly with them. A two-year study of more than twelve thousand adolescents found that the best predictor of health and the strongest deterrent to high risk behavior in teens was a strong connection with at least one adult, at home or at school. This finding held up regardless of family structure, income, race, education, amount of time spent together, where or with whom the child lives, or whether one or both parents work. The message is clear: Good relationships create the resilience that prevents dangerous, acting-out behaviors in our children.

What is sexual health? The World Health Organization defines it as "a positive and respectful approach to sexuality and sexual relationships, as well as the possibility of having pleasurable and safe sexual experiences, free of coercion, discrimination and violence." Don't we all wish exactly this for our children—our sons and our daughters?

A TEEN'S ADVICE

Soon after Jean's daughter, Claudia, turned twenty, she wrote an article for a parenting newsletter about talking with teens about sex. In addition to containing some excellent advice, the article reveals what can happen when children are educated about sex in a positive way during adolescence. Claudia's adolescence wasn't trouble-free (whose is?). She and Jean had plenty of conflict and Jean doesn't feel she handled it well all the time, by a long shot. However, it is clear that Claudia has been able to connect the "boxes in her head" between the family culture and the commercial culture. She is able to look at her experience with perspective and she has developed her own voice for communicating about it, as well as a desire to help others. And she has survived adolescence! Here are excerpts from Claudia's article.

How Parents Can Help Navigate the Rocky Adolescent Road

Whoever says adolescence is the best time of your life doesn't remember being a teenager and/or doesn't know one. Adolescence is rocky and scary and hard. It's a time full of "firsts" and all the excitement but also the pressure that comes with that. Most parents of adolescents feel fear. Fear for their child's safety and development, fear of the choices they'll have to make by themselves and, often times, fear of their child's mood swings and sudden distancing. This is the first time in your child's life that she/he is going out on their own, spending more time away from you than with you, and starting to question everything you say while trusting their friends over you. . . .

One of the big "firsts" that comes with adolescence, and one of the scariest for most parents, is sex. One thing that is necessary to understand right off the bat is that your teen is going to be exposed to sex and sexuality. This doesn't mean they are necessarily engaging in sexual intercourse or even dating, but it means they probably know more than you think they do. They also are unbelievably curious and want to know more. However, learning more from you might be completely mortifying to them, especially if you make a big deal out of talking about sex with them. "The Talk" is no longer the way to go about it. This made more sense in the past when there wasn't so much sex in the media and everywhere around them, and young people were more innocent and less exposed to outside influences. Now, kids have been seeing sexual images (no matter how good your parental controls are) since they were young, and have probably sought out answers from others before coming to you. . . .

Some of my favorite talks with my parents when I was a teenager were when they would tell me about stories from their own adolescence (making sure they were age-appropriate, of course). I read my mother's journals from when she was fourteen when I was fourteen, and I found them fascinating. Your teens may act like they couldn't be less interested in your life. However, chances are that having solid proof (such as stories or documents) showing you went through the same sort of things they are going through will get their attention. Tell them about your first kiss and how nervous you were, how embarrassing it was, etc. Funny or embarrassing stories help remind your kid that you were once their age too, and that the things that seemed mortifying to you at the time are funny now. . . .

It's also very important to remember that sexuality during adolescence isn't always as terrible as the media make it out to be and it very well might not be like that for your teen. There still are loving relationships in which sexual exploration is healthy and normal, and this can be very good for your teen and his or her development. "Firsts" don't always have to be avoided; sometimes they are simply exciting and important for growth.

So before deciding to take drastic measures with your teens to attempt to prevent them or protect them from the dangers of adolescence, talk to them. They're the ultimate resource on what it's like to be a teen in today's world. If you approach them as someone who loves and cares about them and respects them as developing adults, as opposed to someone who's trying to keep them children, you can help. And, even if it doesn't seem like it, they are listening!

Here are some brief pointers on how to talk to your teens about sex:

- Don't go into attack mode. Even if you just found condoms for the first time in your son's closet, don't attack! The only thing you'll get from that is an angry response about how you shouldn't have been in his closet and that you don't respect his privacy. Instead, talk to your teen calmly and ask him or her if he or she needs information about how to be safe, or if the school has been addressing sexual education yet. Don't make it a big deal, just let them know that you are there as a resource if they need you.
- Sometimes it's good to take their advice and back off. If your teens feel cornered or suffocated, they won't tell you anything. They will

retreat and most likely lash out. Make it known that you're there if they want to talk, but don't push it.

• Keep it light. Don't make conversations about sex daunting and stern, but let the topic come and go in normal conversation. This will help your teen realize that you are comfortable with his or her development into adulthood, which will make him or her more likely to trust you.

• Monitor their actions, but from a distance. Making sure you're home when your teen has friends over is good, but making them sit in the living room with you the whole time is not. When I was a teenager and my boyfriend would come over, I knew that my mom was home but she wouldn't constantly check up on us or hover over us. Just knowing that she was there made us more cautious, and knowing she was there made me feel safer. She always said I could use her as an excuse if I felt pressured, and this was comforting to me. Nobody likes feeling pressured, and if you're there and let your teen know that they can use you (even coming up with some sort of a code word with them) as an excuse to get out of something uncomfortable, that will not only help them avoid those situations but it will also make them feel closer to you.

• Ask them questions about their lives. Teens love to talk about themselves, their boyfriends, their girlfriends, and the drama in their friend groups. Why do you think they're on the phone and/or the Internet all the time? If you keep updated on what's going on and ask them direct questions instead of a vague "How was school today?" they will feel like you are genuinely interested and they will start confiding in you more. And please, try not to get judgmental about what they share!

Remember that you were a teen once too, that this does pass, and if you maintain authority but don't try and control them too much your relationship will come out stronger in the end. Also, have fun! Being young is great, and staying connected with your kids as they go through this exhilarating transition will be beneficial for both of you.

Chapter 9

Creating a New
Cultural Environment

You've now been given a comprehensive approach to understand the issues, to counteract harm, and to promote healthy sexual development. However, no matter how hard you try, you can't protect your children completely as long as they live in a toxic cultural environment. It's as if the air were poisoned and you were trying to cope by giving your children masks and keeping all the windows closed in your house. Well, the air *is* poisoned, and although there is a great deal that we can do as individuals, we cannot solve this problem until we act together to change the world our children live in.

We must do this to save not just our own children but also the many children who do not have parents willing or able or equipped to help them. When the corporations say it is all up to parents, what is supposed to happen to these children? We believe we must all work together to make our culture and the world a safer and healthier place for *all* children.

The sexualization of childhood is a public health problem that goes far beyond the home. It affects all of us. And it is increasingly a worldwide phenomenon. The world is fast becoming a global marketplace controlled not by individual governments but by transnational conglomerates interested only in profit and willing to exploit children, even to hijack their sexuality, in pursuit of it.

It is very easy for parents to feel overwhelmed and powerless. We are not powerless. But we must get past the cultural belief, promoted so heavily by advertising, that there is a quick fix, an instant solution to every problem—and that one shouldn't even discuss a problem unless one has this solution firmly in mind. There is no quick fix for the problems discussed in this book, no panacea, but there are many things we can and must do. As Nelson Mandela said, "We must turn this world around—for the children."

As always, the first step is to increase awareness of the problem. We have made great progress in solving other serious and seemingly intractable problems, such as child sexual abuse, intimate partner violence, and drunk driving, by shedding light on them, bringing them into public awareness, encouraging conversation, and sharing our stories and our successes. Until recently, these problems had become "normalized" and therefore were either invisible or ignored or seen as impossible to solve.

As Cordelia Anderson, an expert in the field of child sexual abuse prevention, said, "once something becomes normalized, it becomes the wallpaper of our existence—we don't see it, we accept it as just the way it is and we are numbed to seeing any ill effects or taking action to change it." Philosopher William James put this most succinctly when he said, "What the whole community comes to believe in grasps the individual as in a vise."

New York Times columnist Bob Herbert recently described the normalization of misogyny: "We've become so used to the disrespectful, degrading, contemptuous and even violent treatment of women that we hardly notice it. Staggering amounts of violence are unleashed against women and girls every day. Fashionable ads in mainstream publications play off of that violence, exploiting themes of death and dismemberment, female submissiveness and child pornography."

As we have seen, the sexualization of childhood is being normalized in our culture and throughout the developed world now. As Australian professor Dr. Karen Brooks describes this process, "By gazing at these images, adult consumers are forced to engage in cultural pedophilia: that is, to view under-age girls and boys as sexualized objects whether we want to or not. Our consumption of these images is often passive and uncritical; we're not even aware we're doing it. But, instead of remaining in the realm of visual fiction, these images creep into the everyday language, behavior and dress codes of our children who, desperate to grow up, see them as blueprints for their identity."

We must seize the opportunity to challenge and change this normalization before it becomes even more deeply accepted and expected. We must make the sexualization of childhood socially, economically, politically, and spiritually unacceptable in our nation and the world.

We can learn a great deal from some of the recent successes in changing attitudes about other public health problems, such as those mentioned above. Many of the strategies that have been behind these successes will also work for us. Consider the case of tobacco. About thirty years ago over half of all adult Americans smoked cigarettes. Smoking was allowed in hospitals, movie theaters, just about everywhere. Many airlines offered small packets of cigarettes with meals (many airlines offered *meals*!). Today smoking is not allowed in most public places—including bars in Manhattan, pubs in Dublin, and cafés in Paris, and fewer than 25 percent of adult Americans smoke. This has happened because public health activists worked in many ways to change attitudes about smoking, to ban smoking in public spaces, to prevent children from starting to smoke, and to confront the tobacco industry's manipulative marketing.

These activists also emphasized the positive—clean air, better health, freedom from addiction. We must do the same. Rather than simply decrying the increasing sexualization, we must make it clear what we all stand to gain by changing the environment—such as improved child development, much better relationships between parents and children, lower divorce rates as today's children grow up, a safer world. Although we have to talk about the unhealthy present, our focus should be on a healthy future. What do we want for our children? What positive set of behaviors is most likely to lead to a desirable outcome? How can we create an environment that promotes and supports healthy behaviors, healthy relationships, healthy communities? What is sexual health and how can we help all children to achieve it?

Let's look at some strategies that will make a difference. More detailed information is available from some of the resources listed at the end of this book and on our website.

A DOZEN WAYS TO TURN THE WORLD AROUND

Legislation and Public Policy

1. Regulate marketing to children.

Congress should ban all advertising directed at children. This would not only affect the ads that children see (including those with sexual content), it would affect the shows, games, and toys that fuel these ads. This may seem like a pipe dream, but it is already a reality in some countries. Sweden and Norway have banned all advertising directed at children under the age of twelve, and Greece, Denmark, and Belgium severely restrict advertising aimed at children. At the very least, there should be major restrictions on advertising aimed at children. Commercial speech does not have the same protection as individual free speech under the First Amendment. Advertisements that pose a significant public health risk can be restricted or banned. And the Federal Trade Commission should be given back its power to regulate marketing to children.

2. Require good, clear, coordinated ratings for all programs, video games, and other media.

These ratings must be determined and assigned by authorities outside the industries involved, including child development experts. Public education campaigns should be launched explaining the ratings to parents, because surveys show that many parents do not know much, if anything, about current rating systems. In addition, effective controls must be developed to allow parents much greater ability to block children's access to pornographic websites.

3. Provide federal funding for comprehensive sex education in the schools and accurate, updated sexual health information on government websites.

The government can and should play a vital role in requiring and supporting age-appropriate sex education. Websites should be easy for teens to access. Health organizations and advocacy groups can also provide information on websites.

4. Fund research on the impact of media and marketing and sexualized content on children.

There is currently very little such research, especially on younger children. Private funding needs to be encouraged as well, but funding must not come from industry-connected sources, in order to ensure objectivity and impartiality.

Media

5. Insist that media owners and producers accept some responsibility.

The owners and executives of the major television networks need to recognize that with their free use of the airwaves comes some responsibility to the public. Recording artists and the producers of music videos and video games also need to be more socially responsible. And advertisers must be held accountable for sexist stereotypes and demeaning ads and campaigns. The Federal Communications Commission should take a much more active role in promoting this responsibility, creating standards and holding accountable those who violate them.

Producers of commercial media should be encouraged to provide accurate health information and promote responsible sexual behaviors. Birth control products (including condoms) should be advertised on television. Orchestrated campaigns to encourage the use of seat belts and of designated drivers in television programs have had a positive impact on the behavior of viewers. A number of studies have shown that viewers who watch TV programs with sexual responsibility messages are more likely to be aware of sexual health concerns. Programs that modeled good relationships and positive sexuality would also be helpful!

6. *Use the media to educate the public and draw attention to the problem.*

When tobacco company R. J. Reynolds used a cartoon camel to sell Camel cigarettes to children in the 1980s, the resulting protest eventually succeeded in stopping the campaign. Perhaps more important, it got widespread attention and educated and enraged the public. We need to be creative in dramatizing the damage caused by the sexualization of childhood.

Protests can be effective ways to garner media attention and increase awareness of the issue. Recently a group of thirteen- to sixteen-year-old girls protested Abercrombie & Fitch T-shirts printed with slogans like "Who needs a brain when you've got these?" with a "girl-cott" of A&F that got national news attention. The young women ended up on the *Today* show, and A&F pulled the T-shirts from the stores.

Education

7. *Require accurate, comprehensive sex education in our schools.*

Starting in elementary school, our children should be receiving honest, accurate, age-appropriate sex education that includes skills needed for successful relationships, not just the mechanics of sex. Parenting skills and the basics of early childhood development should also be taught in our schools, as is done in many nations, so that young people will become parents better equipped to deal with their children's needs and to confront the exploitative commercial culture. These programs should be documented to be effective and endorsed by organizations such as the American Academy of Pediatrics. Abstinence-only programs have not met these criteria.

Education alone cannot solve all of the problems created by the sexualization of childhood. But it certainly could help a lot. Today's children pay a much larger price for our refusal to educate them honestly and appropriately about sex than children did before they became fair game for marketers. One in three American girls becomes pregnant before the end of her teen years, far more than in any other developed nation in the world: twice as high as in England and Wales, France and Canada, and nine times as high as in the Netherlands or Japan. One in four sexually active American teens contracts an STD every year, and half of all new HIV infections in this country are among young people.

A 2008 national study found that one-quarter of girls ages fourteen to nineteen were infected with at least one of the four most commonly transmitted STDs. Commenting on this study, Cecile Richards, president of the Planned Parenthood Federation of America, said, "The national policy of promoting abstinence-only programs is a $1.5 billion failure, and teenage girls are paying the real price."

Even if young people escape these consequences, many of them still pay a huge emotional price. Most of the sex education that young people do get teaches them that sex can hurt or kill them but not that it can bring pleasure, joy, and connection. How are they to learn to say "Yes!" in a loving and responsible way? Too many people are afraid of the emerging sexuality of adolescents and respond with rigid rules and futile attempts at control. They seem to believe that sex won't occur to teenagers if it isn't taught in school!

According to Jonathan Klein, chair of the American Academy of Pediatrics Committee on Adolescents, children's best interests are getting lost in the debate over teen sexuality. "We have some groups in our country who would like to prevent unintended pregnancy and sexually transmitted diseases, and some groups that would like to prevent people from having sex." Both are willing to twist research to support their position. Regardless of a parent's opinions about teen sex, he said, more open communication is healthier: "Healthy sexual behavior is part of development. From a medical perspective it's important that parents and children and teenagers are well-educated about the implications of normal psychosocial and sexual development."

Psychologist Michael Milburn, co-author of *Sexual Intelligence*, says, "Both conservatives and liberals have their respective blinders on when talking about teen sexuality. I can think of nothing more important than getting in schools and talking about sexual intelligence and healthy relationships, but most conservatives don't want an open and honest discussion about teen sexuality, and they oppose any conversation that doesn't focus on abstinence until marriage. And many liberals will resist any discussion that might touch on the negative consequences of unbridled sexuality. The conversation we need to have with teens is: What's the role that sexuality should play in an emotionally healthy person's life? What are the different ways that people can be sexual? What are the potential dangers?"

Schools should also implement policies and programs to prevent bullying and sexual harassment and dating violence, and not let the mandate of "No Child Left Behind" crowd social and emotional issues out of the curriculum.

8. Incorporate media education into the school curriculum, starting in the elementary grades.

The United States is one of the few developed nations in the world that does not teach media literacy, but a growing national movement is trying to change that. Organizations such as ACME (Action Coalition for Media Education), the New Mexico Media Literacy Project, and the Media Education Foundation offer materials for parents and teachers.

These days being "literate" requires more than the ability to read and write. We all need to be educated to become critical viewers of the media. The tools of media education enable us to understand, analyze, and interpret, to expose hidden agendas and manipulation, to bring about constructive change, and to further positive aspects of the media. In recent years, there has been increasing understanding of the relationship of media literacy to substance abuse, violence, and other societal problems. Scores of organizations and groups are incorporating media education into their agendas.

Several studies confirm that media literacy programs can "immunize" teens against harmful media effects. Media education has had positive outcomes in preventing violence, eating disorders, and tobacco and alcohol use. It should be a part of every sex education and health education curriculum. Although there has been very little research on the impact of media literacy efforts on younger children, we know that with issues like this one, the earlier we start, the more effective our efforts are likely to be.

There is no better way to learn about something than to try doing it oneself, so most experts agree that media production should be a part of media education. Students can make public service announcements and counter-ads, write op-eds and songs, create blogs and zines and webpages, and make their own films and music videos about sexual health and positive relationships.

Organizations and Coalitions

9. *Join and support organizations working on these issues.*

Join organizations, such as the Campaign for a Commercial-Free Childhood, that work to educate the public, create policies, and demand changes in corporate practices that will support, rather than undermine, people's efforts to be good parents. Diane is a co-founder of this organization, and Jean has worked closely with it for many years. In 2006, CCFC joined forces with Dads & Daughters (another great organization) in a protest against a planned line of dolls based on the Pussycat Dolls (a burlesque female rock group) that was going to be marketed to girls as young as six years old. As a result of the protest, Hasbro did not release the dolls, and many people were made aware of the broader issue of the sexualization of childhood. Many other such organizations are on our resource list.

10. Form coalitions and networks.

We need coalitions, networks, conferences, public outcries. Thirty organizations came together recently to create a coalition to prevent child sex abuse. The range of perspectives include legal, research, policy, community activism, medical, victim services and advocacy, media, education, and more. The mission is "a unified effort to promote the healthy development of children and youth, and end their sexual exploitation."

Many coalitions have formed around other issues, such as high-risk drinking by young people and gang-related violence. Such coalitions not only benefit from the combined expertise of their members but also inspire members to raise the issue and bring prevention efforts into their own organizations. They also encourage public and private organizations to work together and in partnership with communities.

So many issues are related to the sexualization of childhood—child sexual abuse, teen pregnancy, mental health, commercialism and materialism, parenting, and more. All kinds of people can come together around this issue. This is also a way to ensure representation and responsiveness for groups that are often marginalized. We need parents, educators, pediatricians, businesspeople, people in the media, psychologists, the clergy—everyone speaking out and saying, as anchorman Howard Beale so memorably did in Paddy Chayefsky's award-winning film *Network*, "We're as mad as hell and we're not going to take this anymore!"

11. Work politically to create the kind of culture and government that support families and children and make it more difficult for corporations to exploit them.

Using public education campaigns and grassroots organizing, and lobbying for government legislation and policies, we must insist that society (including government and corporations) provide an environment that supports parents' efforts to raise healthy children instead of making their job harder at every turn. Many children don't have the possibility of a strong connection with a parent, so we must make sure they get these connections elsewhere by supporting youth centers, good schools, mentoring programs, and programs to identify children of addicts and other children at risk.

Advocate for effective, age-appropriate sex education programs in schools and oppose federal government efforts to fund abstinence-only sex education programs. Lobby your elected representatives to ensure that government agencies, such as the Federal Communications Commission and the Federal Trade Commission, work to create a healthier cultural environment for children.

These ideas are not abstract ideals or impossible dreams. A recent study of teens in the Netherlands, France, and Germany concluded that "adolescents are valued, respected, and expected to act responsibly. Equally important, most adults trust adolescents to make responsible choices because they see young people as assets rather than problems. That message is conveyed in the media, in school texts, and in health care settings." How different this is from how teens are viewed in this country! We don't lack information about what is necessary to create a healthier environment for our children. What we lack is the political will to achieve it.

12. Find meaningful ways to make a difference, ways that work for you and your family.

There are many ways you can make a difference—with other families, in schools, and in the wider community. Look over our Resources list of organizations working for change, as well as books, films, and other media. See what appeals to you. Cause trouble in whatever way feels appropriate to you—send e-mails, join campaigns, talk to store managers, run for political office. Speak out, speak up, interrupt sexualization when you encounter it. Help your children to become activists too. We can model citizen activism as we work to improve the cultural environment in our communities and throughout the nation and the world. As Mahatma Gandhi said, "We must be the change we wish to see in the world."

TOGETHER WE CAN DO IT

Of course, we can't change overnight all of the problems in society that contribute to the sexualization of childhood. The last thing we want to do is make parents feel even more guilty for not doing a good enough job. Parenting today is hard enough without adding another burden. But every parent can find some way, small or large, to have a voice to advocate for change. Think of the power of our collective voices! As the Canadian singer, songwriter, and activist Raffi, beloved by children in the Western world for many years, said, "You are neither alone, nor a drop in the ocean. You are the ripple, the wave, the gathering swell at a historic turn of the tide."

Acknowledgments

We are very grateful to the parents, teachers, and other professionals who generously shared with us their experiences and stories about coping with today's sexualized childhood. This book would not have been possible without their contributions. They completed questionnaires, participated in interviews, sent e-mails, and more. We greatly respect and appreciate them. Although we can't name them all, we wish to acknowledge a few who made significant contributions: Betty Jane Adams, Cassandra Becker, Del Friedman, Chris Gerzon, Josh Golin, Shelley Kurtz, Lia Lenart, Geralyn McLaughlin, and Stephanie Cox Suarez.

We've been lucky to be guided in this endeavor by three extraordinary and talented women. Jill Kneerim, our incandescent literary agent, understood the importance of this book and why we needed to write it from the moment she first heard about it. Her vision, wisdom, and emotional support were essential. Susan Heath provided crucial editing and organizing advice during the early stages of this project. A literary alchemist, she helped us create a shared voice and a much clearer style. Marnie Cochran, our editor at Ballantine, understands both personally and professionally why parents need this book and how it will help them. We so appreciate her care, attention, and enthusiasm.

Diane gives special thanks to four colleagues who contributed greatly to her motivation to write this book. Twenty-five years ago she and Nancy Carlsson-Paige began a journey exploring how violence, media, and popular culture affect children's development and learning. Kindred spirits, they have written four books together, which helped lay the foundation for many of the ideas expressed here. Gail Dines is a colleague and friend who is deeply committed to promoting justice for women. She and Diane have taught a summer program on media, children, and society at Wheelock College for the past fifteen years. Susan Linn, with whom Diane co-founded the Campaign for a Commercial-Free Childhood, has taught all of us so much about the impact of the commercial culture on children and how to be effective advocates. Finally, Connie Biewald, librarian and growth education teacher at Fayerweather Street School, recognized how the sexualization of childhood was affecting children long before the wider public did. Generously sharing her insights and concerns, she played a key role in getting Diane involved in this topic.

Diane also thanks her colleagues, her students, and the administration at Wheelock College who care so deeply about the well-being of children and families. Gordon Marshall, former president of Wheelock, created the Gordon Marshall Faculty Fellowships, which helped support her work on this book. Wheelock College president Jackie Jenkins-Scott and Susan Pasch, former vice president for academic affairs, offered ongoing appreciation, encouragement, and support. Diane's steering committee colleagues at Teachers Resisting Unhealthy Children's Entertainment (TRUCE) have provided many years of commitment and concern to help parents deal with the media and commercial culture.

Finally, Diane expresses her deepest thanks to her family: her husband, Gary Goldstein, who listened to and valued her hours and hours of talk and work on the book and always believed it would happen; her son, Eli Levin-Goldstein, who grew up in the sexualized and violent media and commercial culture and taught her that there are ways to negotiate the minefields and feel good about where things end up; her parents, who at eighty-eight and ninety-three continue to follow and appreciate her efforts to create a better world for children and families; her sister, Carol, who offers her wisdom on the sexualization of childhood from the point of view of a psychoanalyst; her niece, Julie Russo, who, as a doctoral student in media and cultural studies, provided sage comments on parts of the manuscript; and her nephew Michael Russo, who has always been willing to share his thoughts about the popular culture in his life.

Jean feels very lucky to be affiliated with some wonderful organizations. She especially thanks her friends and colleagues at the Cambridge School of Weston, Lordly & Dame, the Media Education Foundation, the Prevention Research Institute, Teen Talking Circles, and the Wellesley Centers for Women. Thanks also to Frank Baker and Ronit Ridberg for their very helpful research. Jean appreciates the many people in her life who help it run as smoothly as possible, especially Karen Berkley, Bill Cassidy, Peter Culman, Nina Huntemann, Suzanne Kohler, and Diane Wedge.

Jean is very grateful to her treasured friends for their love and support and to all those who have shared their experience, strength, and hope with her over the years. She especially appreciates the help with this book given by Janet Cahaly, Bettie Cartwright, Chris Frost, Tisha Gomes, Connie Holmes, and Mary Lou Shields. She gives special recognition to her old friend Ann Cox Porter, a passionate advocate for children, who died tragically in 2006. She is also grateful to Thomas Lux and Norman and Elinor Lux. She deeply appreciates her family, especially her brothers, Rick, Don, and Jim, and her dazzling daughter, Claudia. And she is always and forever grateful to the late Paul L. Russell.

Finally, we would like to thank each other for the collaboration that has led to this book. Co-writing a book is both a very satisfying and a very challenging endeavor. We have been on an amazing journey together—learning from and supporting each other, finding mutually agreeable solutions to challenges that arose, and finding deep connections between the work on media and gender issues we have been doing independently for so long. The voice we have created together in *So Sexy So Soon* is stronger than either of us could have had on her own—and for this we are extremely grateful.

Resources

For a more complete list of updated resources, with links to websites, please visit www.sosexysosoon.com, www.dianeelevin.com, and www.jeankilbourne.com.

CHILDREN AND THE COMMERCIAL CULTURE

Acuff, D., and R. Reiher. *Kidnapped: How Irresponsible Marketers Are Stealing the Minds of Your Children*. New York: Kaplan Publishing, 2005.

Brooks, K. *Consuming Innocence: Popular Culture and Our Children*. Brisbane: University of Queensland Press, 2008.

Carlsson-Paige, N. *Taking Back Childhood: Helping Your Kids Thrive in a Fast-Paced, Media-Saturated, Violence-Filled World*. New York: Hudson Street Press, 2008.

Levin, D. E. "Compassion Deficit Disorder? Consuming Culture, Consuming Kids, Objectified Relationships." In *Risking Human Security: Attachment and Public Life*, edited by M. Green. London: Karnac Press, 2008.

Levine, M. *The Price of Privilege: How Parental Pressure and Material Advantage Are Creating a Generation of Disconnected and Unhappy Kids*. New York: HarperCollins, 2006.

Linn, S. *Consuming Kids: Protecting Our Children from the Onslaught of Marketing & Advertising*. New York: Anchor Books, 2005.

Olfman, S., ed. *Childhood Lost: How American Culture Is Failing Our Kids*. Westport, CT: Praeger Publishers, 2005.

Palmer, S. *Toxic Childhood: How the Modern World Is Damaging Our Children and What We Can Do About It*. London: Orion Books, 2006.

Quart, A. *Branded: The Buying and Selling of Teenagers*. Cambridge, MA: Perseus Publishing, 2003.

Ravitch, D., and J. Viteritti, eds. *Kid Stuff: Marketing Sex and Violence to America's Children*. Baltimore: The Johns Hopkins University Press, 2003.

Riera, M. *Uncommon Sense for Parents with Teenagers*. Berkeley, CA: Celestial Arts, 1995.

Savage, J. *Teenage: The Creation of Youth Culture*. New York: Viking Adult, 2007.

Schor, J. *Born to Buy: The Commercialized Child and the New Consumer Culture*. New York: Scribner, 2005.

Taylor, B. *What Kids Really Want That Money Can't Buy: Tips for Parenting in a Commercial World*. New York: Time-Warner Books, 2003.

Thomas, S. *Buy, Buy Baby: How Consumer Culture Manipulates Parents and Harms Young Minds*. Boston: Houghton Mifflin, 2007.

Websites

Campaign for a Commercial-Free Childhood (www.commercialfreechildhood.org)

Center for a New American Dream (www.newdream.org). Download a free copy of *Tips for Parenting in a Commercial Culture*.

Teachers Resisting Unhealthy Children's Entertainment (www.truceteachers.org). The *Toy Action Guide* and *Media and Young Children Action Guide* help parents deal with the needs of young children in the commercial culture.

MEDIA AND MEDIA LITERACY

Cantor, J. *"Mommy, I'm Scared": How TV and Movies Frighten Children and What We Can Do to Protect Them*. New York: Harcourt Brace, 1998.

DeGaetano, G. *Parenting Well in a Media Age: Keeping Our Kids Human*. Fawnskin, CA: Personhood Press, 2004.

Dines, G., and J. M. Humez, eds. *Gender, Race and Class in Media: A Text-Reader*. Thousand Oaks, CA: Sage Publications, 2003.

Goodstein, A. *Totally Wired: What Teens and Tweens Are Really Doing Online*. New York: St. Martin's Griffin, 2007.

Kelsey, C. *Generation MySpace: Helping Your Teen Survive Online Adolescence*. New York: Marlowe & Co., 2007.

Kilbourne, J. *Can't Buy My Love: How Advertising Changes the Way We Think and Feel*. New York: Simon & Schuster, 2000.

Levin, D. E. *Remote Control Childhood? Combating the Hazards of Media Culture*. Washington, DC: National Association for the Education of Young Children, 1998.

Media Literacy. Mankato, MN: Capstone Press, 2007 (a series of short books for elementary school students covering movies, music, magazines, television, and online communication).

Rademacher, K. H. *Media, Sex and Health: A Community Guide for Professionals and Parents*. Chapel Hill, NC: The Women's Center, 2007.

Seiter, E. *The Internet Playground: Children's Access, Entertainment, and Mis-education*. New York: Peter Lang Publishing, 2005.

Websites

Action Coalition for Media Education (ACME) (www.acmecoalition.org)

Alliance for a Media Literate America (AMLA) (www.amlainfo.org)

American Academy of Pediatrics (www.aap.org)

Center for Media Literacy (www.medialit.org)

Center on Media and Child Health (www.cmch.net)

Common Sense Media (www.commonsensemedia.org)

Growing Up Online (mediaeducationlab.org)

Henry J. Kaiser Family Foundation (www.kff.org)

Media Education Foundation (www.mediaed.org)

Mind on the Media (www.motm.org)

National Institute on Media and the Family (www.mediafamily.org)

New Mexico Media Literacy Project (www.nmmlp.org)

Teen Media: Mass Media and Adolescent Health (www.unc.edu/depts/jomc/teenmedia/)

POPULAR CULTURE AND GENDER

American Psychological Association Task Force. *Report of the APA Task Force on the Sexualization of Girls.* Washington, DC: American Psychological Association, 2007.

Bishop, M. "The Making of a Pre-pubescent Porn Star: Contemporary Fashion for Elementary School Girls." In *Pop Porn,* edited by A. C. Hall and M. J. Bishop. Westport, CT: Praeger Publishers, 2007.

Brashich, A. *All Made Up: A Girl's Guide to Seeing Through Celebrity Hype . . . and Celebrating Real Beauty.* New York: Walker & Co., 2006.

Cohen-Sandler, R. *Stressed-out Girls: Helping Them Thrive in the Age of Pressure.* New York: Penguin, 2005.

Covington, S. *Voices: A Program of Self-Discovery and Empowerment for Girls.* Carson City, NV: The Change Companies, 2004.

Dee, C. *The Girls' Guide to Life: Take Charge of Your Personal Life, Your School Time, Your Social Scene, and Much More!* Boston: Little, Brown & Co., 2005.

Giananetti, C., and M. Sagarese. *Boy Crazy! Keeping Your Daughter's Feet on the Ground When Her Head Is in the Clouds.* New York: Broadway Books, 2006.

Gruver, N. *How to Say It to Girls: Communicating with Your Growing Daughter.* New York: Prentice Hall Press, 2004.

Katz, J. *Tough Guise: Media Images and the Crisis in Masculinity,* 1999 (a film produced and distributed by the Media Education Foundation).

Kelly, J. *Dads and Daughters: How to Inspire, Understand, and Support Your Daughter When She's Growing Up So Fast.* New York: Broadway Books, 2002.

Kilbourne, J. *Killing Us Softly 3: Advertising's Image of Women,* 2000 (a film produced and distributed by the Media Education Foundation).

Kindlon, D., and M. Thompson. *Raising Cain: Protecting the Emotional Life of Boys.* New York: Ballantine Books, 2000.

Lamb, S., and L. M. Brown. *Packaging Girlhood: Rescuing Our Daughters from Marketers' Schemes.* New York: St. Martin's Press, 2006.

Levine, J. *Harmful to Minors: The Perils of Protecting Children from Sex.* Minneapolis, MN: University of Minnesota Press, 2002.

Levy, A. *Female Chauvinist Pigs: Women and the Rise of Raunch Culture.* New York: Free Press, 2005.

Mysko, C. *Girls Inc. Presents: You're Amazing! A No-Pressure Guide to Being Your Best Self.* Avon, MA: Adams Media Corp., 2008.

Olfman, S., ed. *The Sexualization of Childhood.* Westport, CT: Praeger Publishers, 2008.

Paul, P. *Pornified: How Pornography Is Transforming Our Lives, Our Relationships, and Our Families.* New York: Times Books, 2005.

Pipher, M. *Reviving Ophelia: Saving the Selves of Adolescent Girls.* New York: G. P. Putnam's Sons, 1995.

Pollack, W. *Real Boys: Rescuing Our Sons from the Myths of Boyhood.* New York: Random House, 1998.

Steiner-Adair, C., and L. Sjostrom. *Full of Ourselves: A Wellness Program to Advance Girl Power, Health, and Leadership.* New York: Teachers College Press, 2006.

Zeckhausen, D. *The M.O.D. Squad: A Handbook for Helping Moms Raise Healthy Daughters.* Atlanta: Eating Disorders Information Network, 2007.

Websites

Dads & Daughters (www.dadsanddaughters.org)

Daughters: For Parents of Girls (www.daughters.com)

Geena Davis Institute on Gender in Media (www.thegeenadavisinstitute.org)

Girls Inc. (www.girlsinc.org)

Hardy Girls Healthy Women (www.hardygirlshealthywomen.org/index.php)

Mind on the Media/Turn Beauty Inside Out Project (www.motm.org)

New Moon: The Magazine for Girls and Their Dreams (www.newmoon.org)

PBS Parents Guide to Understanding Girls (www.pbsparents.org/raisinggirls)

SEXUAL DEVELOPMENT AND SEX EDUCATION

For Adults

Blaise, M. *Playing It Straight: Uncovering Gender Discourses in the Early Childhood Classroom.* New York: Routledge, 2005.

Casper, V., and S. Schultz. *Gay Parents/Straight Schools: Building Communication and Trust.* New York: Teachers College Press, 1999.

Chrisman, K., and D. Couchenour. *Healthy Sexuality Development: A Guide for Early Childhood Educators and Families.* Washington, DC: National Association for the Education of Young Children, 2002.

Gordon, S., and J. Gordon. *Raising a Child Responsibly in a Sexually Permissive World.* Avon, MA: Adams Media Corp., 2000.

Linke, P. *Pants Aren't Rude: Responding to Children's Sexual Development and Behavior in the Early Childhood Years.* Watson, ACT, Australia: Australian Early Childhood Association, 1997.

Otis, C. *What's Happening in Our Family: Understanding Sexual Abuse Through Metaphors.* Brandon, VT: Safer Society Press, 2002.

Roffman, D. *Sex and Sensibility: The Thinking Parent's Guide to Talking Sense About Sex.* Cambridge, MA: Da Capo Press, 2001.

———. *But How'd I Get in There in the First Place? Talking to Your Young Child About Sex.* Cambridge, MA: Perseus Publishing, 2002.

For Young Children

Harris, R. H. *It's So Amazing! A Book About Eggs, Sperm, Birth, Babies, and Families.* Cambridge, MA: Candlewick, 1999. (Ages 7 and up.)

———. *Happy Birth Day!* Cambridge, MA: Candlewick, 2002. (Ages 3 and up.)

———. *It's Not the Stork! A Book About Girls, Boys, Babies, Bodies, Families, and Friends.* Cambridge, MA: Candlewick, 2006. (Ages 4 and up.)

For Older Children and Teenagers

Bell, R. *Changing Bodies, Changing Lives: A Book for Teens on Sex and Relationships,* 3rd ed. New York: Three Rivers Press, 1998. (Ages 13 and up.)

Gravelle, K. *The Period Book: Everything You Don't Want to Ask (but Need to Know),* updated edition. New York: Walker Books for Young Readers, 2006. (Ages 10 and up.)

Gravelle, K., N. Castro, C. Chava, and R. Leighton. *What's Going on Down There? Answers to Questions Boys Find Hard to Ask.* New York: Walker Books for Young Readers, 1998. (Ages 9 and up.)

Harris, R. H. *It's Perfectly Normal: Changing Bodies, Growing Up, Sex, and Sexual Health,* updated ed. Cambridge, MA: Candlewick, 2004. (Ages 10 and up.)

Jukes, M. *Growing Up: It's a Girl Thing: Straight Talk About First Bras, First Periods, and Your Changing Body.* New York: Knopf Books for Young Readers, 1998. (Ages 8 and up.)

Maxwell, S. *The Talk: What Your Kids Need to Hear from You About Sex.* New York: Avery, 2008.

Pearson, M. *LoveU2: Comprehensive Relationship Education for Teens.* Berkeley, CA: The Dibble Fund, 2004.

Tolman, D. *Dilemmas of Desire: Teenage Girls Talk About Sexuality.* Cambridge, MA: Harvard University Press, 2002.

Websites

Advocates for Youth (www.advocatesforyouth.org)

Children Now: Talking with Kids About Tough Issues (www.talkingwithkids.org)

Go Ask Alice! Columbia University's health Q&A resource (www.goaskalice.com)

Sex, etc.: Sex Education by Teens, for Teens (www.sxetc.org)

Teen Aware: Sex, Media and You (www.teenawareresources.org)

Teenwire.com (www.teenwire.com; run by Planned Parenthood)

Notes

Introduction: Changing Times, Changing Needs, Changing Responses

3 **"Baby, I'm your slave. I'll let you whip me if I misbehave":** From the Justin Timberlake song "SexyBack" on the album *FutureSex/LoveSounds,* Jive Records, 2006.

3 **Halloween costumes for young girls are so suggestive:** M. Philips, "Eye Candy: Little Girls' Halloween Costumes Are Looking More Like They Were Designed by Victoria's Secret Every Year. Are We Prudes or Is This Practically Kiddie Porn?" *Newsweek* Web Exclusive, October 29, 2007 (retrieved November 1, 2007, from www.newsweek.com/id/62474/output/print).

4 **Some of the students said they were playing "the rape game":** J. Saltzman and M. Tench, "5 at Elementary School Suspended," *Boston Globe,* A1, A9, May 20, 2006.

4 **For instance, younger children have Bratz dolls:** MGA Entertainment press release, "BRATZ Becomes No. 1 in Fashion Themed Dolls and Accessories in the USA," February 5, 2007 (retrieved April 10, 2007, from www.mgae.com/downloads/pressreleases/Bratz%20Press%20Release.pdf).

9 **A 2003 *Newsweek* story on the rapid rise in teen prostitution:** S. Smalley, "This Could Be Your Child," *Newsweek,* August 18, 2003.

9 **According to the most reliable studies, as many as one in three girls:** J. Briere and D. M. Elliott, "Prevalence and Psychological Sequelae of Self-reported Childhood Physical and Sexual Abuse in a General Population Sample of Men and Women," *Child Abuse and Neglect,* 27 (2003): 1205–22.

9 **Almost 90 percent of the time:** D. Finkelhor, H. Hammer, and A. Scdlak, "Sexually Assaulted Children: National Estimates and Characteristics," *Juvenile Justice Bulletin* (Washington, DC: Office of Juvenile Justice & Delinquency Prevention, 2008).

11 **Around the same time that Diane taught her course:** J. Kilbourne, *Killing Us Softly: Advertising's Image of Women* (film) (Cambridge, MA: Cambridge Documentary Films, 1979).

Chapter 1: Never Too Young to Be Sexy

15 **A 2002 survey by an organization called Public Agenda:** "A Lot Easier Said Than Done: Parents Talk About Raising Children in Today's America," www.public agenda.org, 2002 (retrieved October 23, 2003, from www.publicagenda.org/research/research_reports_details.cfm?list=15).

16 **Several recent books and news and research reports:** For instance, see Benoit Denizet-Lewis, "Friends, Friends with Benefits and the Benefits of the Local Mall," *New York Times Magazine,* May 30, 2004, and A. Jones and M. Miley, *Restless Virgins: Love, Sex and Survival at a New England Prep School* (New York: William Morrow, 2007).

20 **Nora was aware of a 2006 Kaiser Family Foundation report:** V. Rideout and E. Hamel, *The Media Family: Electronic Media in the Lives of Infants, Toddlers, Preschoolers and Their Parents* (Menlo Park, CA: Henry J. Kaiser Family Foundation, May 2006).

23 **A highly publicized story about a first-grader:** R. Ranalli and R. Mishra, "Boy's Suspension in Harassment Case Outrages Mother," *Boston Globe,* A1, Section: Metro/Region, February 8, 2006.

29 **As James Baldwin said, "Not everything that is faced can be changed":** Quoted in E. Smith, "Race and Responsibility," *Reason,* May 1995 (retrieved online at www.reason.com/news/show/29681.html).

Chapter 2: From Barbie to Bratz and Beyond

31 **They know how to get children to nag their parents to buy them things:** Western Media International and Lieberman Research Worldwide reported the study *The Fine Art of Whining: Why Nagging Is a Kid's Best Friend* in 1998. (Western Media International is now called Initiative Media Worldwide.)

34 **The Henry J. Kaiser Family Foundation has done a series of invaluable annual reports:** V. Rideout, E. Vandewater, and E. Wartella, *Zero to Six: Electronic Media in the Lives of Infants, Toddlers and Preschoolers* (Menlo Park, CA: Henry J. Kaiser Family Foundation, October 2003).

35 **Since the 2003 report came out, there has been an even bigger push to lure infants to the screen:** D. Oldenburg, "Experts Rip 'Sesame' TV Aimed at Tiniest Tots: Producers Defend DVD's as Right for Under 2s," *Washington Post,* C1, March 21, 2006.

35 **A 2005 Kaiser Family Foundation Report surveyed the screen habits:** D. F. Roberts, U. G. Foehr, and V. Rideout, *Generation M: Media in the Lives of 8–18-Year-Olds* (Menlo Park, CA: Henry J. Kaiser Family Foundation, March 2005).

35 **They are exposed to an average of forty thousand ads per year:** "American Academy of Pediatrics Policy Statement on Children, Adolescents, and Advertising," *Pediatrics,* December 2006.

35 **More than 80 percent of popular teen TV shows:** D. Kunkel, E. Biely, K. Kyal, et al., *Sex on TV 3* (Menlo Park, CA: Henry J. Kaiser Family Foundation, 2003).

35 **a 1978 Federal Trade Commission report concluded:** Federal Trade Commission, *Staff Report on Television Advertising to Children* (Washington, DC: Government Printing Office, 1978).

36 **(a conclusion that the American Psychological Association reiterated in 2004):** *Report of the APA Task Force on Advertising and Children* (Washington, DC: American Psychological Association, February 20, 2004).

36 **This successful campaign not only stopped Congress:** N. Minow and

C. LaMay, *Abandoned in the Wasteland: Children, Television, and the First Amendment* (New York: Hill & Wang, 1995).

36 Until the mid-1980s, children's television was regulated: D. E. Levin and N. Carlsson-Paige, *The War Play Dilemma: What Every Parent and Teacher Needs to Know,* 2nd ed. (New York: Teachers College Press, 2006).

36 The first blockbuster show after deregulation was *Masters of the Universe*: See the monthly bestselling toy sales figures in *Playthings* magazine (the periodical of the Toy Industry Association of America) from 1985 through 1986.

36 Around the same time, most of the networks that aired children's programming: T. Englehardt, "Saturday Morning Fever: The Hard Sell Takeover of Kids' TV," *Mother Jones,* 11 (1986): 38–48, 54.

37 In 1990, after intense lobbying efforts: Minow and LaMay, *Abandoned in the Wasteland.*

37 Second, and more alarmingly in terms of exposing kids: N. Carlsson-Paige and D. E. Levin, *Who's Calling the Shots: How to Respond Effectively to Children's Fascination with War Play and War Toys* (Gabriola Island, BC: New Society Publishers, 1990).

38 Around this time, teachers began reporting: Levin and Carlsson-Paige, *The War Play Dilemma.*

38 Boys were more involved in play with violent themes: N. Carlsson-Paige and D. E. Levin, "The 'Mighty Morphin Power Rangers': Teachers Voice Concern," *Young Children,* September 1995.

38 A KFF report from a year earlier: V. J. Rideout, *Parents, Media and Public Policy: A Kaiser Family Foundation Survey* (Menlo Park, CA: Henry J. Kaiser Family Foundation, September 2004).

39 Video game industry sales of almost $18 billion in 2007: B. Ortutay, "Nintendo Tops Video Game Sales in 2007," Associated Press, January 17, 2008.

41 When the *Transformer* movie came out: www.toysrus.com (information retrieved on August 10, 2007).

43 One Ralph Lauren ad in *The New York Times: New York Times,* April 18, 2004.

46 "It's hard to have a brand for kids": Interview with Lynne Neary, "Tweens and Media: What's Too Adult?" *All Things Considered,* National Public Radio, August 1, 2006.

47 According to one survey, about 40 percent of Internet users: T. DeAngelis, "Children and the Internet: Web Pornography's Effect on Children," *Monitor on Psychology,* 38, no. 10 (November 2007): 50.

47 There's an emotional health issue at stake: Ibid.

50 However, the degree to which most adults trust Disney: For a detailed critique of gender issues in Disney movies, see the documentary film *Mickey Mouse Monopoly: Disney, Childhood and Corporate Power* (Northampton, MA: Media Education Foundation, 2001).

50 Disassociate sex from non-market feelings: C. Peters, "G-strings for Seven-Year-Olds! What's a Parent to Do?" *Znet Commentary,* November 2, 2002 (retrieved online at www.zmag.org/sustainers/content/2002=11/02peters.cfm).

Chapter 3: Sexual Development Derailed

54 What follows here is a list of key characteristics: For more detailed information about sexual development and young children, see K. Chrisman and D. Couchenour, *Healthy Sexuality Development: A Guide for Early Childhood Educators and Families* (Washington, DC: National Association for the Education of Young Children, 2002).

57 **Looking at children through a developmental lens:** For more information about young children's thinking, see D. Singer and T. Revenson, *A Piaget Primer: How a Child Thinks,* revised ed. (Madison, CT: International Universities Press, 1997).

61 **Joanne Cantor, in her book "*Mommy, I'm Scared*":** J. Cantor, *"Mommy, I'm Scared": How TV and Movies Frighten Children and What We Can Do to Protect Them* (New York: Harcourt Brace, 1998).

63 **Eileen Zurbriggen, the chair of the American:** American Psychological Association, *Report of the APA Task Force on the Sexualization of Girls* (Washington, DC: APA, 2007).

66 **Children of today are living a remote control childhood:** D. E. Levin, *Remote Control Childhood? Combating the Hazards of Media Culture* (Washington, DC: National Association for the Education of Young Children, 1998).

67 **The resulting condition can be called "problem-solving deficit disorder":** Diane originally coined the term "Problem Solving Deficit Disorder" in 2003 to capture concerns she heard from parents and professionals about how media were impacting children's play, creativity, and imagination.

Chapter 4: The Toll on Parents, Families, and Schools

73 **For example, in September 2001:** Diane co-founded the Campaign for a Commercial-Free Childhood (www.commercialfreechildhood.org) in 2000 and is currently a member of the steering committee. Jean has been involved with CCFC almost since the beginning.

74 **The headline on the ad company's press release proclaimed:** The study was conducted by Western Media International (now Initiative Media Worldwide) in 1998. For more information see S. Linn, *Consuming Kids: Protecting Our Children from the Onslaught of Marketing and Advertising* (New York: Anchor, 2005).

75 **In a 2002 survey of parents of five- to seventeen-year-olds:** Public Agenda, "A Lot Easier Said Than Done: Parents Talk About Raising Children in Today's America," www.publicagenda.org, 2002 (retrieved October 23, 2003).

80 **Twelve Reasons Why Just Saying No Isn't Enough:** Adapted with permission from Levin, *Remote Control Childhood?*

82 **And *The Washington Post* reported:** B. Schulte, "For Little Children, Grown-up Labels as Sexual Harassers," *Washington Post,* April 3, 2008 (retrieved at www.washingtonpost.com/wp-dyn/content/story/2008/04/02/ST2008040203589).

Chapter 5: Helping Children Through the Minefields

92 **A Crash Course on Media Rating Systems:** Adapted from the TV Parenting Guidelines Monitoring Board (information retrieved January 8, 2008, at www.tvguidelines.org/ratings.asp).

93 **Video, Computer, and Internet Game Ratings:** Adapted from the Entertainment Software Ratings Board (ESRB) (information retrieved January 8, 2008, at www.esrb.org/ratings/ratings_guide.jsp).

93 **Movie Ratings:** Adapted from the Classification and Rating Administration (CARA) (information retrieved January 8, 2008, at www.filmratings.com).

102 *Provide toys:* For a more detailed discussion of media-linked toys and play, see Levin and Carlsson-Paige, *The War Play Dilemma.*

105 **Suggest they act out some aspect of a book you read to them:** M. Sendak, *Where the Wild Things Are* (New York: HarperCollins, 1963).

108 **WHAT YOU CAN DO To Create a Give-and-Take Process:** Adapted from Levin, *Remote Control Childhood?*

Chapter 6: Working It Out Together

125 **More and more children are viewing Internet pornography** "Study: More Kids Exposed to Online Porn: 42 Percent of Internet Users Ages 10–14 Have Viewed Sexual Images," Associated Press, February 5, 2007 (retrieved March 5, 2007, from www.msnbc.msn.com/9d/16981028).

Chapter 7: The Sexualized Child Enters Adolescence

138 **Matt was playing *Grand Theft Auto*:** Ad track, *USA Today,* 2B, December 31, 2007.

139 **Although the federal government spends more than $175 million:** G. Harris, "Teen Births Increase for 1st Time [in] 15 Years," *Boston Globe,* December 6, 2007 (retrieved online at www.boston.com/news).

140 **Teenagers spend $155 billion a year:** A. Quart, *Branded: The Buying and Selling of Teenagers* (Cambridge, MA: Perseus Publishing, 2003).

140 **Teenage girls spend over $8 billion annually:** L. Parks, "Chains Court Teen Shoppers as Cosmetic Customers," *Drug Store News,* September 7, 1998. In *Report of the APA Task Force on the Sexualization of Girls* (Washington, DC: American Psychological Association, 2007), 24 (retrieved September 3, 2006, at www.findarticles.com/p/articles/mi_m3374/is_n14_v20/ai_21147316).

140 **sex has long been used in advertising:** This topic is discussed in much greater depth in Jean's film series *Killing Us Softly: Advertising's Image of Women* and in her book *Can't Buy My Love.*

140 **The ad for an energy drink called "Pimp Juice":** C. Anderson and S. Cooper, "Countering Harmful Social Trends: Actions to Prevent the Impact from Normalization of Sexual Harm and Child Sexual Exploitation," in *Preventing Sexual Violence and Exploitation: A Sourcebook,* ed. K. Kaufman (Oklahoma City: Wood 'n' Barnes Publishing, 2008).

142 **In 2003, girls between the ages of thirteen and seventeen:** A. Pollet and P. Hurwitz, "Strip Till You Drop: Teen Girls Are the Target Market for a New Wave of Stripper-Inspired Merchandise," *The Nation,* January 12, 2004, 20.

142 **In one study, more than one-third of middle-school students:** V. O'Connell, "Fashion Bullies Attack—in Middle School," *Wall Street Journal,* October 25, 2007, D1.

143 **One movie critic, writing about *American Pie*:** O. Glieberman, "Virgin Megascore," *Entertainment Weekly,* July 16, 1999, 43–44, quoted in V. Strasburger, "Adolescents, Sex, and the Media: Ooooo, Baby, Baby," *Adolescent Medicine,* 16 (2005): 269–88 (reference #2).

143 **In the prizewinning 2004 film *Me and You and Everyone We Know*:** J. Brody, "Children, Media and Sex: A Big Book of Blank Pages," *New York Times,* January 31, 2005 (retrieved online at www.nytimes.com).

143 **Twelve percent of all websites are pornography sites:** APA, *Sexualization of Girls,* 11.

143 **Lauren Phoenix, star of scores of porn films:** M. Morford, "Porn Stars in My Underwear," SFGate.com, June 24, 2005 (retrieved online at www.SFGate.com).

143 **Jenna Jameson has launched her own fashion line:** M. E. Babej and T. Pollak,

"Mad Ave Goes Soft Porn," *Forbes,* October 4, 2006 (retrieved online at www.forbes.com).

143 **"The Internet gives teen boys the idea":** Quoted in Denizet-Lewis, "Friends, Friends with Benefits and the Benefits of the Local Mall."

144 **A popular Facebook group called "Thirty Reasons":** "Facebook Group Celebrates Drunk Young Women," Join Together News Summary, December 12, 2007 (retrieved online at www.jointogether.org) (originally reported on CNN December 10, 2007).

144 **MySpace, a site for tweens and young teens:** L. Deeley, "I'm Single, I'm Sexy, and I'm only 13," *The Times,* July 28, 2007 (retrieved online at www.timeson line.co.uk).

144 **One study of twenty-one covers of popular young women's magazines:** A. R. Malkin, W. Kimberlie, and J. C. Chrisler, "Women and Weight: Gendered Messages on Magazine Covers," *Sex Roles,* 40 (1999): 647–55.

145 **One study of the effects of listening to popular music:** S. M. Martino, R. L. Collins, M. N. Elliott, A. Strachman, D. E. Kanouse, and S. H. Berry, "Exposure to Degrading Versus Nondegrading Music Lyrics and Sexual Behavior Among Youth," *Pediatrics,* 118 (August 2006): 430–41. See also J. D. Brown, K. L. L'Engle, C. J. Pardun, G. Guo, K. Kenneavy, and C. Jackson, "Sexy Media Matter: Exposure to Sexual Content in Music, Movies, Television, and Magazines Predicts Black and White Adolescents' Sexual Behavior," *Pediatrics,* 117, no. 4 (April 2006): 1018–27.

146 **well-known directors of pornographic films:** J. Richard, "Selling Sex to Kids," *Toronto Sun,* July 17, 2005 (retrieved online at www.torontosun.com).

146 **Two-thirds of young people . . . have TVs in their bedrooms:** Brody, "Children, Media and Sex: A Big Book of Blank Pages." See also D. F. Roberts, U. G. Foehr, V. J. Rideout, and M. Brodie, *Kids and Media at the New Millennium: A Comprehensive National Analysis of Children's Media Use* (Menlo Park, CA: Henry J. Kaiser Family Foundation, November 1999).

147 **One in four American children . . . five or more TVs:** Roberts, Foehr, and Rideout, *Generation M: Media in the Lives of 8–18-Year-Olds,* 9.

147 **Indeed, the number of sexual scenes:** K. H. Rademacher, *Media, Sex and Health: A Community Guide for Professionals and Parents* (Chapel Hill, NC: The Women's Center, 2007), 10.

147 **Seventy percent of all TV programs contain sexual content:** D. Kunkel, K. Eyal, K. Finnerty, E. Biely, and E. Donnerstein, *Sex on TV 4: A Kaiser Family Foundation Report* (Menlo Park, CA: Henry J. Kaiser Family Foundation, November 2005), 20.

147 **Almost all of this sexual activity is consequence-free:** KFF, *Sex on TV 4.* See also J. D. Brown, B. S. Greenberg, and N. L. Buerkel-Rothfuss, "Mass Media, Sex and Sexuality," in *Adolescent Medicine: Adolescents and the Media,* ed. V. C. Strasburger and G. A. Comstock (Philadelphia: Hanley & Belfus, 1993).

147 **The vast majority of children and adolescents play video games:** H. Paik, "The History of Children's Use of Electronic Media," in *Handbook of Children and the Media,* ed. D. G. Singer and J. L. Singer (Thousand Oaks, CA: Sage, 2007), 7–27; in APA, *Sexualization of Girls,* 10.

147 **Games made both for home systems and for computers:** T. L. Dietz, "An Examination of Violence and Gender Role Portrayals in Video Games: Implications for Gender Socialization and Aggressive Behavior," *Sex Roles,* 38 (1998): 425–42, in APA, *Sexualization of Girls,* 10.

147 **Young people today spend an average of nearly six and a half hours:** KFF, *Generation M: Media in the Lives of 8–18-Year-Olds,* 39.

Notes

148 **The few studies that do exist:** Brown et al., "Sexy Media Matter." See also R. L. Collins, M. N. Elliott, S. H. Berry, D. E. Kanouse, D. Kunkel, S. B. Hunter, and A. Miu, "Watching Sex on Television Predicts Adolescent Initiation of Sexual Behavior," *Pediatrics,* 114, no. 3 (September 2004): e280–89.

148 **In general, key communications theories:** V. C. Strasburger, " 'Clueless': Why Do Pediatricians Underestimate the Media's Influence on Children and Adolescents?" *Pediatrics,* 117, no. 4 (April 2006): 1427–32.

148 **So although most of the messages about sex in the media:** Committee on Public Education, "Sexuality, Contraception, and the Media," *Pediatrics,* 107 (2001): 191–94.

149 **the media function as a kind of *super peer:*** J. D. Brown, C. T. Halpern, and K. L. L'Engle, "Mass Media as a Sexual Super Peer for Early Maturing Girls," *Journal of Adolescent Health,* 36, no. 5 (May 2005): 420–27.

149 **One study found that three out of four fifteen- to seventeen-year-olds:** Kaiser Family Foundation, *Teens, Sex and TV* (Menlo Park, CA: Henry J. Kaiser Family Foundation, 2002).

149 **However, another survey of teenagers:** Rademacher, *Media, Sex and Health,* 12.

149 **In a survey of more than two thousand teenage girls:** P. Haag, *Voices of a Generation: Teenage Girls on Sex, School, and Self* (Washington, DC: American Association of University Women Educational Foundation, 1999).

149 **As pediatrician and media expert Victor Strasburger says:** "Adolescents, Sex, and the Media: Ooooo, Baby, Baby," 273–74.

150 **University of North Carolina researcher Jane Brown:** Brown et al., "Sexy Media Matter."

150 **The average American teenager views nearly fourteen thousand:** K. H. Rademacher, *Media, Sex and Health,* 10.

150 **Brown found that white adolescents:** Brown et al., "Sexy Media Matter."

150 **As Brown said, "If you believe *Sesame Street* taught":** J. D. Brown, "Decency, Indecency and Community Standards," *Talk of the Nation.* National Public Radio, February 9, 2004.

150 **Two studies with older children:** Collins et al., "Watching Sex on Television." See also S. Clark, R. L. Nabi, and E. Moyer-Gusé, "Television Consumption and Young Women's Expectations of Sexual Timing," paper presented at International Communication Association Conference, San Francisco, May 2007. Printed in *Media Report to Women* (Summer 2007): 4–12.

150 **A study by the Rand Corporation:** Martino et al., "Exposure to Degrading versus Non-Degrading Music Lyrics."

150 **Another study found that young black girls:** S. H. Peterson, G. M. Wingood, R. J. DiClemente, K. Harrington, and S. Davies, "Images of Sexual Stereotypes in Rap Videos and the Health of African American Female Adolescents," *Journal of Women's Health,* 16, no. 8 (October 2007): 1157–64.

150 **Dr. Brown faults media portrayals:** J. D. Brown, B. S. Greenberg, and N. L. Buerkel-Rothfuss, "Mass Media, Sex and Sexuality," in *Adolescent Medicine: Adolescents and the Media,* ed. Strasburger and Comstock.

151 **Although the sexual sell, overt and subliminal:** Kilbourne, *Can't Buy My Love,* 263.

151 **As French philosopher Roland Barthes said:** R. Barthes, *The Empire of Signs* (1970), quoted in E. White, "From Albert Camus to Roland Barthes," *New York Times,* September 12, 1982, section 7, page 1.

152 **Roughly half of all fifteen- to nineteen-year-olds:** *National Youth Risk Behavior Survey, 1991–2005. Trends in the Prevalence of Sexual Behaviors* (Atlanta:

Centers for Disease Control and Prevention, 2006). See also L. S. Stepp, "Oral Sex Prevalent Among Teens, Study Says," *Boston Globe*, A3, September 16, 2005.

152 **They refer to these encounters as "hooking up":** Denizet-Lewis, "Friends, Friends with Benefits and the Benefits of the Local Mall."

152 **They can end up like the twenty-two-year-old client:** B. F. Meltz, "'FWB'Trend Distorts the Lessons of Sex and Love," *Boston Globe,* October 21, 2004, H1, H5.

152 **One male college student described the "hookup culture":** J. Reitman, "Sex and Scandal at Duke," *Rolling Stone,* June 1, 2006 (retrieved online at www.rollingstone.com).

152 **teenage girls . . . become clinically depressed:** D. D. Hallfors, M. W. Waller, D. Bauer, C. A. Ford, and C. T. Halpern, "Which Comes First in Adolescence— Sex and Drugs or Depression?" *American Journal of Preventive Medicine,* 29, no. 3 (October 2005): 163–70.

153 **most teenage pregnancies begin:** B. G. Reed, "Linkages: Battering, Sexual Assault, Incest, Child Sexual Abuse, Teen Pregnancy, Dropping Out of School and the Alcohol and Drug Connection," in *Alcohol and Drugs Are Women's Issues,* ed. P. Roth (Metuchen, NJ: Scarecrow Press, 1991): 130–49.

153 **Alcohol and other mind-altering drugs permit sexual activity:** The relationship of alcohol, gender, and sexuality is explored in one of Jean's films, *Spin the Bottle: Sex, Lies and Alcohol* (Northampton, MA: Media Education Foundation, 2004), and in her first book, *Can't Buy My Love: How Advertising Changes the Way We Think and Feel.*

154 **They attend parties on college campuses:** Reitman, "Sex and Scandal at Duke."

154 **College students willingly flash their breasts:** A. Pollet and P. Hurwitz, "Strip Till You Drop: Teen Girls Are the Target Market for a New Wave of Stripper-Inspired Merchandise," *The Nation* (January 12, 2004), 20.

155 **"It's kind of like domination through sex":** Reitman, "Sex and Scandal at Duke."

155 **Donna Lisker, director of Duke University's women's center:** Ibid.

155 **Eight students were suspended from a Virginia high school:** T. Bahrampour and I. Shapira, "Sex at School Increasing, Some Educators Say," *Washington Post,* C01, November 6, 2005.

155 **As columnist Maureen Dowd said:** M. Dowd, "What's Up, Slut?" *New York Times,* July 15, 2006 (retrieved online at www.nytimes.com).

155 **Even if girls repeatedly get the message:** *The Report of the APA Task Force on the Sexualization of Girls* (Washington, DC: American Psychological Association, 2007).

155 **Other research has found that this self-objectification:** B. L. Frederickson et al., "That Swimsuit Becomes You: Sex Differences in Self-Objectification, Restrained Eating, and Math Performance," in APA, *Sexualization of Girls,* 23. See also N. M. McKinley, "Women and Objectified Body Consciousness: Mothers' and Daughters' Body Experiences in Cultural, Developmental, and Familial Context," in APA, *Sexualization of Girls,* 23; M. Tiggeman, and A. Slater, "A Test of Objectification Theory in Former Dancers and Non-Dancers," in APA, *Sexualization of Girls,* 23.

156 **A study of ninth-grade girls:** D. L. Borzekowski, T. Robinson, and J. D. Killen, "Does the Camera Add 10 Pounds? Media Use, Perceived Importance of Appearance, and Weight Concerns Among Teenage Girls," *Journal of Adolescent Health,* 26 (2000): 36–41, in Strasburger, "Adolescents, Sex, and the Media," 280.

156 **Another found that watching music videos of girl bands:** E. Connolly, "Girl Bands Damage Teenagers," Sydney *Sunday Telegraph,* June 10, 2007.

156 **girls . . . who . . . wanted to look like television or movie stars:** A. E. Field,

L. Cheung, A. M. Wolf, et al., "Exposure to the Mass Media and Weight Concerns Among Teenage Girls," *Pediatrics,* 103 (1999): e236, in Strasburger, "Adolescents, Sex, and the Media," 281.

156 **More than two-thirds of girls . . . influenced by the fashion magazines they read:** Ibid.

156 **Although larger body types are acceptable:** Rademacher, *Media, Sex and Health,* 15.

157 **Girls with physical disabilities:** APA, *Sexualization of Girls,* 27.

157 **The pressure on young women:** This has been documented more fully by Jean in her *Killing Us Softly: Advertising's Image of Women* film series and her book *Can't Buy My Love.*

157 **young women today feel tremendous pressure to be *perfect*:** Reitman, "Sex and Scandal at Duke." See also Girls Inc., "The Supergirl Dilemma: Girls Feel the Pressure to Be Perfect, Accomplished, Thin, and Accommodating" (retrieved October 12, 2006, www.girlsinc.org/supergirldilemma).

157 **Girls are twice as likely as boys:** National Institute of Mental Health, reported by A. Johnson, "Is Her World Safe and Fair?" *Daughters,* November/December 2007, 15.

157 **Between 2003 and 2004 the suicide rate for girls:** K. M. Lubell, S. R. Kegler, A. E. Crosby, and D. Karch, *Morbidity and Mortality Weekly Report,* 56, no. 35 (September 7, 2007): 905–8 (published by the Centers for Disease Control and Prevention, Atlanta).

157 **The single group of teenagers most likely to consider suicide:** C. E. Martin, "Rethinking Antidepressants and Youth Suicide," *AlterNet,* September 25, 2007 (www.alternet.org/story/62971).

157 **A girl who has negative feelings about her body:** G. Wingood and R. DiClemente, "Culture, Gender and Psychosocial Influences on HIV-Related Behavior of African Female Adolescents: Implications for the Development of Tailored Prevention Programs," in APA, *Sexualization of Girls,* 27.

157 **And she may well have sexual problems in adulthood:** APA, *Sexualization of Girls,* 26.

158 **Media violence has not only increased in quantity:** Rademacher, *Media, Sex and Health,* 15.

158 **Nearly half of American high school students have had sexual intercourse:** S. L. Escobar-Chaves, S. R. Tortolero, C. M. Markham, B. J. Low, P. Eitel, and P. Thickstun, "Impact of the Media on Adolescent Sexual Attitudes and Behaviors," *Pediatrics,* 116 (2005): 303–26.

158 **Far more disturbing, however, is:** Committee on Public Education, "Sexuality, Contraception, and the Media," *Pediatrics,* 107 (2001): 191–94.

158 **Nine out of ten girls . . . pressure about sex:** *The Kaiser Family Foundation and Seventeen National Survey of Teens About Sex: Gender Roles* (Menlo Park, CA: Henry J. Kaiser Family Foundation, December 2002).

158 **Forty-one percent . . . unwanted sex:** M. J. Blythe, D. Fortenberry, M. Temkit, T. Wanzhu, and D. P. Orr, "Incidence and Correlates of Unwanted Sex in Relationships of Middle and Late Adolescent Women," *Archives of Pediatrics and Adolescent Medicine,* 160 (June 2006): 591–95.

158 **National research suggests . . . sexually abused:** C. T. Halpern, S. G. Oslak, M. L. Young, S. L. Martin, and L. L. Kupper, "Partner Violence Among Adolescents in Opposite Sex Romantic Relationships: Findings from the National Longitudinal Study of Adolescent Health," *American Journal of Public Health,* 91 (2001): 1679–85. See also J. G. Silverman, A. Raj, L. A. Mucci, and J. E. Hathaway, "Dating Violence Against Adolescent Girls and Associated Substance Use,

Unhealthy Weight Control, Sexual Risk Behavior, Pregnancy, and Suicidality," *Journal of the American Medical Association,* 286 (2001): 372–79.

159 **frequent exposure to media with highly sexualized imagery:** J. Ward, "The Skin We're In: Teaching Our Teens to Be Socially Smart, Emotionally Strong and Spiritually Connected," in APA, *Sexualization of Girls,* 27. See also L. M. Ward and R. Rivadeneyra, "Contributions of Entertainment Television to Adolescents' Sexual Attitudes and Expectations: The Role of Viewing Amount Versus Viewer Involvement," in APA, *Sexualization of Girls,* 27; E. L. Zurbriggen and E. M. Morgan, "Who Wants to Marry a Millionaire? Reality Dating Television Programs, Attitudes Toward Sex, and Sexual Behaviors," in APA, *Sexualization of Girls,* 27.

159 **girls and young women who watch a lot of "reality" TV:** Zurbriggen et al., "Who Wants to Marry a Millionaire?" in APA, *Sexualization of Girls,* 27.

159 **Men who are frequent readers of men's magazines:** L. M. Ward, A. Merriwether, and A. Caruthers, "Breasts Are for Men: Media Use, Masculinity Ideology, and Men's Beliefs About Women's Bodies," in APA, *Sexualization of Girls,* 31.

159 **Men exposed to sexualized content:** J. S. Strouse, M. P. Goodwin, and B. Roscoe, "Correlates of Attitudes Toward Sexual Harassment Among Early Adolescents," in APA, *Sexualization of Girls,* 31–32. See also L. M. Ward, "Does Television Exposure Affect Emerging Adults' Attitudes and Assumptions About Sexual Relationships? Correlational and Experimental Confirmation," in APA, *Sexualization of Girls,* 31–32; L. M. Ward and K. Friedman, "Using TV as a Guide: Associations Between Television Viewing and Adolescents' Sexual Attitudes and Behavior," in APA, *Sexualization of Girls,* 31–32.

159 **For both boys and girls . . . stronger acceptance of sexual harassment:** Strouse et al., "Correlates of Attitudes Toward Sexual Harassment Among Early Adolescents," in APA, *Sexualization of Girls,* 34.

159 **African American teenage girls exposed to sexualized rap videos:** J. D. Johnson, M. S. Adams, L. Ashburn, and W. Reed, "Differential Gender Effects of Exposure to Rap Music on African American Adolescents' Acceptance of Teen Dating Violence," in APA, *Sexualization of Girls,* 27–28.

160 **According to the APA report mentioned earlier:** APA, *Sexualization of Girls,* 35.

161 **A 2008 study:** A. Smiler, " 'I Wanted to Get to Know Her Better': Adolescent Boys' Dating Motives, Masculinity Ideology, and Sexual Behavior," *Journal of Adolescence,* 31, no. 2 (February 2008): 17–32.

161 **the importance of attachment:** D. Brooks, "Of Human Bonding," *New York Times,* July 2, 2006 (retrieved online at www.nytimes.com).

162 **As George Gerbner . . . said:** G. Gerbner, "Television Violence: The Art of Asking the Wrong Question" (July 1994), in *The World & I: A Chronicle of Our Changing Era,* 385 (retrieved online from the Center for Media Literacy, www.medialit.org/reading_room/article459.html), and quoted in S. Stossel, "The Man Who Counts the Killings," *Atlantic Monthly,* May 1997 (retrieved online at www.theatlantic.com).

163 **As cultural anthropologist Margaret Mead once said:** In a speech at Richland College, Dallas, February 24, 1977.

Chapter 8: Helping Teenagers Through the Minefields

164 **As researcher Kate Rademacher says:** Rademacher, *Media, Sex and Health,* 42.

165 **nearly two-thirds of teenagers say they have a TV in their bedroom:** Roberts, et al., *Kids and Media at the New Millennium.*

165 **parents' views can override depictions in the media:** Strasburger, "Adolescents, Sex, and the Media," 283; also, Brown et al., "Sexy Media Matter."

167 **University of North Carolina researcher Jane Brown:** Brown et al., "Sexy Media Matter."

167 **"Just say 'later' ":** Strasburger, " 'Clueless': Why Do Pediatricians Underestimate the Media's Influence on Children and Adolescents?" 1428.

172 **half the parents who say their kids are not sexually experienced are wrong:** T. L. Young and R. Zimmerman, "Clueless: Parental Knowledge of Risk Behaviors of Middle School Students," *Archives of Pediatrics and Adolescent Medicine,* 152 (November 1998): 1137–39.

172 **58 percent of middle school students were . . . sexually active:** Strasburger, 'Clueless.'

173 **As parents, the most important thing we can do for our children:** Kilbourne, *Can't Buy My Love,* 312.

173 **A two-year study of more than twelve thousand adolescents:** C. Dooley and N. Fedele, "A Response to the Columbine Tragedy," *Connections* (Jean Baker Miller Training Institute, Wellesley Centers for Women, Spring 1999), 2.

173 **The World Health Organization defines [sexual health] as:** H. Boerner, "Cancer Vaccines, Birth Control, Emergency Contraception: With All These Options, Are Teens Any Sexually Healthier?" *San Francisco Chronicle,* CM13, February 11, 2007.

174 **How Parents Can Help Navigate the Rocky Adolescent Road:** C. K. Lux, "A Teen's Advice: How Parents Can Navigate the Rocky Adolescent Road." *The Parent Buzz* (Planned Parenthood League of Massachusetts parent e-newsletter, September 2007; retrieved at www.plannedparenthood.org/ma/parent-buzz-sept-2007.html).

Chapter 9: Creating a New Cultural Environment

178 **But we must get past the cultural belief:** Kilbourne, *Can't Buy My Love,* 292.

178 **As Nelson Mandela said:** In a speech at the launch of the Say Yes to Children campaign in 2000, quoted by Raffi Cavoukian in *My Hero: Extraordinary People on the Heroes Who Inspire Them* (New York: Free Press, 2005), 164.

178 **Cordelia Anderson, an expert in . . . child sexual abuse prevention:** C. Anderson and S. Cooper, "Countering Harmful Social Trends: Actions to Prevent the Impact from Normalization of Sexual Harm and Child Sexual Exploitation," in *Preventing Sexual Violence and Exploitation: A Sourcebook,* ed. K. Kaufman (Oklahoma City: Wood 'n' Barnes Publishing, 2008).

178 **Philosopher William James:** William James, "The Moral Equivalent of War," Lecture 11 (1906), in *Memories and Studies* (New York: Longman Green and Co., 1911), 289.

178 ***New York Times* columnist Bob Herbert:** B. Herbert, "Misogyny Is America's True National Pastime," *New York Times,* January 17, 2008 (retrieved online from AlterNet, www.alternet.org/story/74004/).

179 **Australian professor Dr. Karen Brooks:** K. Brooks, "Corporate Kidnapping," *Sydney's Child,* December 2005 / January 2006, 19.

179 **We must make the sexualization of childhood . . . unacceptable:** National Coalition to Prevent Child Sexual Abuse, *National Plan to Prevent Child Sexual Exploitation,* draft, January 9, 2008, 3.

179 **public health activists worked . . . to change attitudes about smoking:** Jean was actively involved in the campaign against the tobacco industry from the beginning. She began lecturing about tobacco advertising in the late 1970s and made a film, *Pack of Lies: The Advertising of Tobacco,* in 1992 (remade in 2004 as *Deadly Persuasion: The Advertising of Alcohol and Tobacco*). She discussed tobacco advertising in depth in her first book, *Can't Buy My Love.*

180 **Let's look at some strategies that will make a difference:** These strategies and others are discussed in greater depth in Jean's first book, *Can't Buy My Love.*.

180 **Sweden and Norway have banned all advertising directed at children:** Committee on Communications, "Children, Adolescents, and Advertising," *Pediatrics,* 118 (2006): 2563–69. For more information on this issue, see S. Linn, *Consuming Kids: Protecting Our Children from the Onslaught of Marketing & Advertising* (New York: Anchor Books, 2005).

181 **The owners and executives of the major television networks:** Strasburger, " 'Clueless': Why Do Pediatricians Underestimate the Media's Influence on Children and Adolescents?" 1429.

182 **TV programs with sexual responsibility messages:** Ibid. See also Kunkel et al., *Sex on TV 4: A Kaiser Family Foundation Report.*

182 **protested Abercrombie & Fitch T-shirts:** Pennsylvania Coalition Against Rape (Enola, PA), "Girlcott Puts Abercrombie Tees in Cold Storage," *PCAR Pinnacle,* Spring 2006, 7, 11.

183 **These programs should be documented to be effective:** Strasburger, "Clueless," 30.

183 **One in three American girls becomes pregnant:** Kunkel et al., KFF, *Sex on TV 4.*

183 **One in four sexually active American teens:** Ibid.

183 **A 2008 national study found that one-quarter of girls:** L. Altman, "Sex Infections Found in Quarter of Teenage Girls," *New York Times,* March 12, 2008, A1 and A17.

183 **Even if young people escape these consequences:** Kilbourne, *Can't Buy My Love.*

183 **sex can hurt or kill them:** N. Bernstein, "Learning to Love," *Mother Jones,* January/February 1995, 45–49, 54.

184 **According to Jonathan Klein:** Quoted in "In the United States," *Washington Post,* May 16, 2006 (retrieved at www.washingtonpost.com/wp=dyn/content/article/2006/05/15/AR2006051500826.html).

184 **Psychologist Michael Milburn:** Quoted in Denizet-Lewis, "Friends, Friends with Benefits and the Benefits of the Local Mall."

185 **the relationship of media literacy to . . . societal problems:** Jean was the first person to use media literacy for prevention of a wide variety of public health problems, including violence against women, eating disorders, high-risk drinking, and tobacco use. She began this work in the late 1960s. She has lectured extensively and internationally on these issues for more than thirty-five years and has made several films and published many articles and one book.

185 **media literacy programs can "immunize" teens:** Strasburger, "Adolescents, Sex, and the Media," 284. See also J. D. Brown, "Media Literacy Has Potential to Improve Adolescents' Health," *Journal of Adolescent Health,* 39, no. 4 (2006): 459–60.

185 **Media education has had positive outcomes:** Kunkel et al., KFF, *Sex on TV 4.*

185 **the impact of media literacy efforts on younger children:** For more information on media literacy with young children, see Levin, *Remote Control Childhood?* Other media literacy resources are listed in Resources.

186 **Thirty organizations came together:** C. Anderson, *Progress Report on the National Coalition to Prevent Child Sexual Exploitation,* National Center for Missing and Exploited Children, June 27, 2007, 3.

187 **A recent study of teens in the Netherlands, France, and Germany:** M. A. Kelly and M. McGee, "Report from a Study Tour: Teen Sexuality Education in The Netherlands, France, and Germany," *SIECUS Report,* 27 (1999): 11–14, in Strasburger, "Adolescents, Sex, and the Media," 283.

188 **"We must be the change"**: M. K. Gandhi, quoted in P. L. Walker, "The Significance of Gandhi's Thoughts to the Problems of the 21st Century," paper presented at "Gandhi in the 21st Century: A Symposium," Northwestern University Kellogg School of Management, October 2, 2001.

188 **Canadian singer, songwriter, and activist Raffi**: R. Cavoukian and S. Olfman, *Child Honoring: How to Turn This World Around* (New York: Praeger Publishing, 2006), 241. We are grateful to Cordelia Anderson for bringing this to our attention.

Index

ABOUT THE AUTHORS

DIANE E. LEVIN, PH.D., is a professor of education at Wheelock College in Boston, where she has been involved in training early childhood professionals for more than twenty-five years. An internationally recognized expert who helps professionals and parents deal with the effects of violence, media, and commercial culture on children, Levin is a senior adviser to the PBS parents' website for girls, the co-founder of the Campaign for a Commercial-Free Childhood, and the author or co-author of six other books, including *Remote Control Childhood?* and *The War Play Dilemma* (co-author). She is a frequent keynote speaker and workshop presenter, and has been a guest on many radio and television programs. She lives in Cambridge, Massachusetts.

JEAN KILBOURNE, ED.D., is internationally recognized for her pioneering work on alcohol and tobacco advertising and the image of women in advertising. *The New York Times Magazine* named her one of the three most popular speakers on college campuses. Her award-winning films include the *Killing Us Softly* series, *Slim Hopes, Calling the Shots,* and *Spin the Bottle.* The author of *Can't Buy My Love: How Advertising Changes the Way We Think and Feel,* she is a frequent guest on radio and television programs such as *Today* and *The Oprah Winfrey Show.* She has testified before the U.S. Congress and has been an adviser to two surgeons general. A Senior Scholar at the Wellesley Centers for Women, Kilbourne lives in Newton, Massachusetts.

ABOUT THE TYPE

This book was set in Fairfield, the first typeface from the hand of the distinguished American artist and engraver Rudolph Ruzicka (1883–1978). In its structure Fairfield displays the sober and sane qualities of the master craftsman whose talent has long been dedicated to clarity. It is this trait that accounts for the trim grace and vigor, the spirited design and sensitive balance, of this original typeface.

Rudolph Ruzicka was born in Bohemia and came to America in 1894. He set up his own shop, devoted to wood engraving and printing, in New York in 1913 after a varied career working as a wood engraver, in photoengraving and banknote printing plants, and as an art director and freelance artist. He designed and illustrated many books, and was the creator of a considerable list of individual prints—wood engravings, line engravings on copper, and aquatints.